CW01336557

Gold Investment Book

James Marsh

BLACKWELL
JEWELLERS

"While the presses for fiat currency may keep running, it's the gold that truly keeps the world turning."

Table of Contents

Foreword 5
   By David Godfrey - Perfection Jewellery Ltd

Introduction 7
   By James Marsh

Chapter 1 12
   The Big battle

Chapter 2 29
   A Brief History of Gold

Chapter 3 45
   The Birth of The Central Bank

Chapter 4 62
   The National Debt is Soaring!

Chapter 5 82
   The Sad Reality of Our Political System

Chapter 6 97
   China's Gold Rush

Chapter 7 112
   CBDC (Central Banks Digital Currency)

Chapter 8 128
   Property vs. Precious Metals

Chapter 9 141
   The Intensity of the Wealth Transfer: It's No Joke!

Chapter 10 153
   Silver Fox

Chapter 11 164
   How NOT to Invest in Gold

Chapter 12 181
    Gold: The Best Investment You'll Ever Make

Chapter 13 192
    Let's Talk About Storing

Chapter 14 203
    Do You Believe in Luck?

Chapter 15 216
    Final Thoughts

Chapter 16 221
    A Little Gift From Me!

Foreword

I first met James Marsh about 15 years ago, thanks to Mehmet, the owner of a well-respected jewellery shop in Sutton.

At the time, James had been handling Mehmet's repairs in his own workshop for a couple of years, and Mehmet thought I should supply jewellery to James' shop.

James had poured most of his savings into preparing and fitting out his shop, leaving him with limited funds to spend on stocking up.

From the very beginning, it was clear he was a likeable, determined chap, and we were more than happy to help him out with an extended credit deal.

James began his journey in the jewellery industry by opening his shop in Gravesend, Kent amid the last financial crisis.

Despite the economic hardships that came with those times, he managed to establish a highly successful retail business.

His positive attitude towards business, coupled with his unwavering determination to excel in all he does, has been the drive behind his accomplishments.

Over the years, he's proven himself to be an innovative force in the jewellery world, consistently coming up with fresh, state-of-the-art ideas.

He's created a myriad of exclusive collections, and his infectious enthusiasm is simply unmatched. In my long career,

I've had the pleasure of working with only a handful of people who possess the same boundless energy as James.

Now, James has set his sights on giving back to the industry that's brought him so much success. He's on a mission to protect the future of the jewellery trade by inspiring and nurturing the next generation.

To achieve this, he's developed a series of comprehensive online courses that will, step by step, impart the wealth of manufacturing knowledge he's amassed over the years.

Whether passionate about the art of jewellery making, a budding jeweller looking to hone your skills, or a seasoned professional seeking to expand your knowledge, you can be confident you're learning from the best in the business.

With his guidance, expertise and support, you'll learn the ins and outs of the jewellery trade, and gain invaluable skills that will set you up for a successful career in this fascinating industry.

There's no better time than the present to improve your outlook on life, and James' courses offer the perfect opportunity to embark on this enriching journey.

I've no doubt his teachings will leave a lasting impact on you and on the industry, paving the way for the next generation of jewellery artisans to thrive and flourish.

I sincerely hope you'll take advantage of this golden opportunity to refine your craft and become a part of the exciting future of the jewellery industry.

As someone who's had the privilege of working closely with James, I can attest to his steadfast commitment to excellence, his passion for the craft, and his genuine desire to help others succeed.

The jewellery world is truly fortunate to have someone like James Marsh leading the charge to preserve its future and nurture the talent of tomorrow.

- **David Godfrey**, *Perfection Jewellery Ltd*

Introduction

Hello, my name is James Marsh. Before we delve into a brief history of gold, let me give you a quick backstory about myself and how this precious metal has contributed to my financial success.

You see, I've been crafting jewellery for over 30 years, and I now have three successful jewellers based in Kent. It's taken me two decades of sheer hard work to reach this point. I'm not saying this to show off, but rather to demonstrate that having gold, and silver, in your corner, or as part of your portfolio, can help offset inflation and serve as a fantastic safe haven in the world of investment.

Let's rewind to 1990—before the internet was a thing, and when mobile phones were larger than house bricks. I wasn't the best student in the world, and I left school with no qualifications. I just didn't enjoy it, and don't even get me started on being told what to do! I was always more at ease trying to make money in the playground. I loved art, and it was something I naturally gravitated towards. However, I always had to be the class clown and was soon removed from lessons, opting to be in the lower groups with my mates.

Towards the end of my school years, I'd skive off lessons, flog stuff from my bedroom, and then hit the arcade games or fruit machines. I didn't have a plan when I left school, and after a few interviews, I still had no real direction.

Then, one sunny day, I was on my usual jaunt to the arcades when I passed a small jewellery store. I looked up and saw a sign asking for a full-time jewellery polisher. By this time, I was feeling the pressure from my mum to get a job, and the reality was sinking in that the world doesn't owe you anything. I needed to get a job and earn some money.

As mentioned earlier, it was 1990, and things were different. I walked into the store, expressed my interest, and before I knew it, I was given a trial run and had landed my first job. Now let me tell you, making jewellery is no glamorous gig. When you think of diamonds, adverts paint a glossy picture, but in a jewellery workshop, that couldn't be further from the truth. Polishing was a filthy job; I'd come home looking like I'd spent days up a chimney.

To make matters worse, I was bullied for being small for my age, and my boss was a right swine. He and the foreman would stick my head down the toilet and flush, or wrap silver wire around my fingers and heat it up. I suppose these were just the usual trials an apprentice had to endure. But one thing that truly helped was my boss' exceptional knowledge of traditional jewellery making, which I absorbed like a sponge.

I struggled for the first three years, and looking back, I think I was a nervous wreck with all the belittling and constant put-downs. But I stuck it out. I also decided to bulk up and stand up for myself more. So at 18, I hit the gym—something that's stayed with me for over 30 years. It's one of the main things that's kept me on track.

After about five years, my artistic flair started to break through, and I began gaining respect, having gone from a 9-stone weakling to a 13-stone weightlifter. I stuck with it until I was 26, when I realised this job wasn't taking me anywhere. My earnings had peaked, and the only way I could see myself becoming successful was by setting up my own business.

I couldn't just up and leave; I needed a plan. After all, I had a mortgage and dreams of starting a family—things that require a steady cash flow. But deep down, I knew I could make it work. So I set about getting everything in place. I figured I needed about £1,000 worth of jewellery trade work to cover the costs of a small unit, all the overheads, and leave me with a wage I was accustomed to. But with the added benefit of growth and, hopefully, one day owning my own store.

At the time, I didn't have my own premises, so I needed to create the illusion that I had an established business. I reached out to jewellers across the UK to see if I could secure enough trade work to make my exit. I sent out over 100 letters, and after a few weeks, I followed up with all the potential clients. The results weren't outstanding, but after persistent calls, I managed to secure work from one shop, then another, and before I knew it, I had five shops on board.

I didn't tell my boss about this private work, but when he saw the list of materials I was using, he cottoned on to my plan. That's when everything changed. Things got uncomfortable, so I decided to leave. I didn't quite have enough work, but at least now I had more time to pitch to potential clients.

My first year in my workshop went better than planned. My hard work paid off, and I even hired my first employee, Michael, who's still with me today. It took me three years to open my first store just outside Gravesend town; I didn't have the funds for a prime location yet. But with another three years of graft and buying gold, I eventually made it happen.

You see, when the banks collapsed in 2007, the price of gold skyrocketed, and that's when the gold rush began. After another three years, I'd saved enough money to buy my dream store in Bexleyheath—prime location, baby! That was 2012.

Over the next eight years, I built up a stockpile of gold and a loyal customer base. Along the way, I also grew my property portfolio, using my business as a vehicle to invest in real estate. With the price of gold rising, it helped generate even more money.

Then 2020 rolled around and COVID-19 struck. I don't need to tell you what that did to the world, but one thing's for sure: gold prices reached new heights. I figured now was a perfect time to create a workbook about the history of gold, how it can help offset inflation and shed light on currency manipulation—and how excessive money printing during the pandemic created a dangerously fragile bubble. I hope you find it engaging, insightful and, above all, enjoyable.

Happy reading!

- *James Marsh*

"Gold is the lifeblood of the economy, it pulses with value that outlives all paper promises."

Chapter 1

The Big Battle

"James's Fun Facts"

"Ever heard of the 'Gold Standard'?

It's not just a fancy term. It's when countries tied the value of their currency to gold.

Britain started this trend in 1821. Always setting those trends, aren't we?"

Chapter 1: The Big Battle

Our Ever-Changing Battle

Let's embark on a journey back in time. Throughout the ages, society has always grappled with a battle, though often unseen. It's not the type of battle you'd see on a historic battlefield, with clashing swords and valiant knights.

Instead, it's an economic battle that's silently fought in the background of our everyday lives. And while most of us might be busy getting on with life, the effects of this battle are felt deep in our wallets.

How many times have you gone shopping, only to be taken aback by the sudden spike in prices?

Maybe it was that loaf of bread you purchase every week or the butter you spread on your toast every morning. Or perhaps it was the monthly utility bill, which seemed to have sprung a few extra digits out of nowhere.

Life seems to have a funny way of becoming more expensive when we least expect it. You pull up to the petrol station, and there's an unexpected hike in fuel prices. Your monthly bills begin to resemble intimidating mountain ranges.

And in the midst of all this, platforms like Only Fans, once seen as affordable entertainment, are hiking their prices too—though, of course, I only know this from a friend.

But here's the kicker—amidst this financial vise, you're left with no choice. These aren't luxuries but necessities. And for these necessities, you need to pay.

A Glimpse into Ancient Wallets

Would you believe me if I told you that once upon a time, chickens, cows, and even exotic spices doubled up as money?

It's fascinating, and somewhat amusing, to imagine a world where someone might pay for a house with a herd of goats or buy a garment with a sack of peppercorns.

These commodities, albeit unconventional by today's standards, were the currencies of the past. But before we delve deeper, let's debunk a common misconception.

Cash Isn't Always King

We're often told, "Cash is king." But what if I told you that's not entirely accurate?

When someone hands you a £20 note, your immediate instinct is to equate it with money. But there's a twist. While all money can act as a currency, not all currency is money.

Let's break this down. Currency is essentially a medium—a tool we use to trade. You give someone a piece of currency, like a £10 note, and in return, you receive something of value. It's like a promise, a token that represents a certain worth.

But if we examine the £10 note itself, its intrinsic value is almost negligible. It's just a piece of polymer, after all. I fondly recall my grandparents slipping me a £1 note during the holidays. Back then, it felt like a treasure. Today, it's barely enough for a cup of coffee.

However, this doesn't render our £10 note useless. Because, while it might lack intrinsic value, it holds purchasing power. It's this power that enables you to exchange it for tangible assets, like a gram of gold, which has real, intrinsic value.

The Glitter of Gold

Having established the subtle difference between money and currency, let's shift our focus to a substance that has been at the centre of human desire for millennia: gold.

When an investor speaks of dabbling in currencies, they might refer to the buying and selling of, say, euros or Japanese yen, anticipating these will rise or fall in value compared to their own currency.

But when they mention investing in money, more often than not, they're talking about gold—either in bars or coins. And unlike the ever-fluctuating nature of fiat currencies, gold has an inherent value.

Central banks can't whimsically decide to produce more gold; it's a finite resource.

Unravelling the Mystery of Fiat Currency

But let's backtrack a bit. What's this "fiat currency" I mentioned?

Hold on to your hats, because this might ruffle a few feathers.

Your beloved pound, dollar, or euro? It's not truly worth the paper (or polymer) it's printed on.

A fiat currency is a type of currency that's not anchored to a physical commodity like gold or silver. Its value is derived from the trust and confidence of the people who use it—essentially, it's worth what the government says it's worth.

Sounds a bit precarious, doesn't it?

Believe it or not, the concept of using such abstract value markers is relatively new in the grand tapestry of human history. Societies of yore relied on physical commodities like gold and silver as money.

There's a certain simplicity and assurance in this system. After all, there's only so much gold or silver in the world, ensuring you can't just conjure up more of it on a whim, safeguarding the economy from runaway inflation.

The shift towards a world dominated by fiat currencies was gradual. A prominent turning point was the 20th century, when the U.S. dollar, which was initially backed by precious metals, began its transition into the world of fiat.

By the time 1971 rolled around, the gold standard had been abandoned, and the dollar became a pure fiat currency.

And it wasn't just the dollar. As the years rolled by, nations across the globe embraced fiat currencies, leaving the era of commodity-backed money largely in the annals of history.

Continuing from where we left off:

The Crafty Government Ploy with Fiat Currency

Now, I don't want to sound conspiratorial, but have you ever paused to ponder why governments are so keen on championing fiat currencies? What do they stand to gain?

When we had a gold or silver standard, there was a limit to how much money a government could mint or print.

There was a tangible cap, and it kept things in check. But with fiat currencies, the rules of the game changed. Now, governments had the liberty to print more money whenever they felt the need. Seems convenient, doesn't it?

The harsh reality is that this convenience comes at a cost, and more often than not, it's the average Joe and Jane that foot the bill.

The Silent Thief: Inflation

Imagine waking up one day to find that your savings have shrunk—not because someone broke into your bank, but because the very money itself has diminished in value. Sounds bizarre, right? Yet, this happens more often than we realize, and it's got a name: inflation.

Inflation, in the simplest terms, is the rate at which the general level of prices for goods and services rises, causing purchasing power to fall. When inflation rates soar, every unit of currency buys fewer goods and services.

So, if you've been wondering why that candy bar seems to shrink a little bit every year while its price inches up, you've got inflation to blame.

And what fuels inflation? A significant driver is the overproduction of money by central banks—printing more than what's sustainable or needed.

But it's not just about the quantity of money; it's about the demand and supply of goods and services in the market, too.

How Gold Shines Amidst Inflation

Gold has often been regarded as a safeguard, a shield against the ravages of inflation. But why is that?

You see, gold is scarce. It's not something you can produce in abundance at the drop of a hat. And this very scarcity, coupled with its universal appeal, gives it an edge over volatile fiat currencies.

When inflation surges, and fiat currencies start losing their charm, investors flock to gold, seeing it as a more stable and trustworthy store of value. This isn't just speculation—it's backed by history.

During periods of economic uncertainty or high inflation, the price of gold has often surged It stands as a beacon of stability amidst the stormy seas of fluctuating currency values.

The Deception Behind the Curtain

There's a grim side to the world of fiat currency that often remains veiled. Every time the government prints more money without backing or genuine need, it dilutes the value of the currency already in circulation.

Remember the principle of demand and supply?

Too much supply without corresponding demand devalues a product, or in this case, currency.

It's a bit like being part of a magic trick where the magician makes your money disappear, bit by bit. Only, it's not magic—it's policy. And the slight of hand? It's called quantitative easing. A fancy term for a simple act: creating money from thin air.

While it sounds like something out of a fairy tale, it's a tactic central banks, like the Bank of England, employ. They mint new currency and lend it to the government at interest. And guess who's left picking up the tab? You guessed it—it's us, the unsuspecting public.

Grappling with an Imposed System

It's not just about stealthy tactics or policies that chip away at our wealth. There's a more direct approach governments employ to ensure the dominance of their fiat currency: legislation.

In many nations, alternative forms of currency are illegal. Even in places where they aren't, laws dictate that taxes can only be paid using the official fiat currency.

It's a bit like being in a game where the rules are rigged from the start. You're forced into a system, whether you trust it or not.

The Tantalizing Appeal of Gold

Throughout history, civilizations have venerated gold. The ancient Egyptians saw it as a symbol of divinity, the Incas referred to it as the "tears of the Sun", and for the Romans, it was the embodiment of wealth and power.

But why?

Why this yellow metal?

Gold's charm isn't just skin deep. Beyond its gleaming façade, gold has properties that make it uniquely suited for currency and value storage:

Durability: Unlike food or livestock, gold doesn't rot or degrade. A gold coin from ancient Greece still shines with the same lustre today.

Divisibility: Gold can be divided into smaller portions without losing its value. Ten smaller gold pieces have the same total weight, and hence value, as one large piece.

Portability: A small amount of gold can represent a large amount of monetary value, making it easy to carry and store.

Uniformity: Each piece is equivalent to another of the same weight and purity.

Limited Supply: Gold can't be manufactured or printed. It has to be mined and refined, which makes it scarce, thereby driving up its value.

Fiat Currency: The Allure and the Pitfall

In direct contrast to gold, fiat currency does not have intrinsic value. Its worth is not based on a physical commodity but rather the trust and credit of the economy. Now, trust is a beautiful thing, but it's also fragile.

The strength of fiat currencies, their flexibility, is also their Achilles' heel. Governments can easily adjust their monetary policies, print more money, and manoeuvre economic levers to respond to financial crises.

But every time they print more currency without a corresponding increase in goods and services, the value of each unit of that currency diminishes.

Why Central Banks Love Gold

You might find it surprising, but central banks, the very institutions that issue fiat currency, are among the world's largest holders of gold.

As of the last data cut-off, central banks held over 33,000 tonnes of gold, about one-fifth of all the gold ever mined. Why this paradox?

Gold provides these institutions with diversification. It acts as a hedge against inflation and currency fluctuations. In times of economic downturns, when confidence in fiat currency wavers, gold remains steadfast.

Moreover, gold is universally accepted and can be used to trade or settle debts between countries. In a world rife with economic uncertainties and fluctuating exchange rates, gold offers a stable touchpoint.

Fiat's Tryst with Trust

At the heart of the fiat system lies trust. It's trust in the government, trust in the economy, and trust in the institutions that uphold these structures. But as history has shown, trust can be betrayed.

Hyperinflation in Zimbabwe or the Weimar Republic in Germany are glaring examples of this breach. In these scenarios, the unchecked printing of money led to catastrophic consequences with currency becoming practically worthless.

The Gold Standard: A Blast from the Past

Before fiat took the world by storm, many countries operated on the gold standard. It was a system where the value of a country's money was directly linked to a specific amount of gold.

This system ensured that governments couldn't just conjure money out of thin air. They could only mint as much currency as they had gold to back it up.

While the gold standard offered stability, it was rigid. It tied the hands of policymakers, preventing them from using monetary policies to address economic challenges, ultimately leading to its abandonment in favour of the more flexible fiat system.

But as we stand on the crossroads of economic uncertainties, with digital currencies like Bitcoin making waves, one can't help but wonder: is a return to some form of gold standard on the horizon? Or will we forge a new path, blending the best of gold, fiat, and digital currencies?

Unravelling the Fiat Fabric

When you hold a £10 note in your hand, it feels palpable, tangible. It feels real. But the truth is, its value isn't in the paper or the intricate designs. Its value is a belief system, an elaborate promise that society collectively upholds.

Currency vs Money: This is where the distinguishing line between currency and money becomes clear. A £10 note isn't valuable in itself.

But gold, a physical asset with intrinsic worth, does not rely on collective belief. It holds value because of its tangible properties and scarcity, not because of an overarching societal agreement.

Central Banks and the Magic Show

Central banks have an influential role in the world of fiat currency. With the power to dictate monetary policy and interest rates, they can influence the value of currency significantly. But, like every magician, they rely on distractions and illusions.

Quantitative Easing: This fancy term essentially means the process where a central bank buys government securities or other securities from the market to increase the money supply.

The aim?

To lower interest rates and boost spending. But every time this is done, the purchasing power of existing money in circulation gets slightly eroded. Like adding water to pure juice, the value gets diluted.

The Mirage of Security

We, as individuals, feel a sense of security when we look at our bank statements and see a good amount of money saved up.

But let's unravel this a bit. Your savings are essentially a number in a digital ledger, a promise from a bank that you have 'X' amount of value stored with them.

Now, in stable economies, this system works seamlessly. You trust the bank, the bank trusts the government, and the government has faith in its monetary policies.

But the chain is as strong as its weakest link. If any segment of this chain falters, the illusion can shatter.

The True Impact of Inflation

Inflation, at its core, is about balance – or rather, the lack of it. It's the consequence of having more money chasing after the same, or fewer, goods and services.

While mild inflation is often seen as a sign of a growing economy, unchecked inflation can be disastrous.

The Silent Thief: Inflation is often dubbed the 'silent thief'.

Why?

Because it quietly erodes the value of your money.

If you saved £100 last year and there's an inflation rate of 10% this year, your £100 is effectively only worth £90 in terms of purchasing power.

Gold's Unyielding Power: When inflation is high, tangible assets like gold come to the forefront. Gold doesn't rely on the fragile balance of trust in the system.

It's a refuge, a bastion against the turbulent seas of economic uncertainty.

When the value of currency wanes due to inflation, the relative value of gold, being finite and tangible, often stands resolute.

A World Without Fiat?

Imagining a world without fiat currency might seem outlandish. But let's indulge in this thought experiment.

If fiat currencies, with all their flexibility and flaws, were to disappear tomorrow, what would the world look like?

We'd revert to barter systems, or perhaps a new form of trade currency would emerge, rooted in tangible assets. The intrinsic value of items would take centre stage, and the abstract concept of 'trust in the system' would diminish.

However, entirely dismissing the fiat system would be naïve. For all its flaws, it has facilitated global trade, bridged economies, and fostered innovation.

The key might not be in discarding it, but in refining it, ensuring that the system's checks and balances prevent the pitfalls we've witnessed in the past.

James's Chapter Summary for the Busy Bee (Or a Quick Recap)

🌐 World of Wealth 101:

Picture this: There's a tug-of-war between two heavyweights—sparkling gold and paper money (fiat currency).

💡 Trust is Everything:

Fiat monies like that friend who promises to pay you back: We all believe it has value, until one day... it might not.

When governments print too much money (because, why not?), things can go haywire (Zimbabwe and Weimar Republic, we're looking at you).

✨ Gold's Ancient Fan Club:

Egyptians: "Gold is divine!" Incas: "It's the Sun's tears!" Romans: "We're rich!"

Why? Gold's cool qualities: it doesn't spoil, you can break it without losing value, it's easy to carry, every piece is the same, and it's rare.

🏦 Banks' Golden Secret:

Fun fact: The very banks pushing paper money? They're hoarding gold like it's going out of fashion.

📜 Gold Standard Rewind:

Once upon a time, countries had a golden rule: their money's worth was based on gold. No stash of gold? No printing money!

Though it sounded like a dream, it was pretty restricting. Think of it as the economy's straightjacket. Too tight for comfort!

🚀 Enter: Digital Cash:

Bitcoin's on the scene, making us wonder: Gold 2.0? Or just another player in the money game?

💸 Money vs. REAL Money:

Holding a £10 note? Feels real. But it's just a fancy IOU.

Gold doesn't play that game. It's solid, tangible, and doesn't rely on Pinky promises.

🎩 Central Banks: Masters of Illusion:

These banks? Like magicians with fancy terms. "Quantitative Easing" = adding more money, but also diluting its value.

⚖️ Inflation: The Sneaky Thief:

Inflation's that sneaky mate quietly taking chips off your plate. Your savings? They're buying less than before.

Gold, on the other hand, just chills and stays strong.

💭 Futuristic Thought Bubble:

A world without paper money? Madness? Maybe. But if fiat went poof, we'd probably be bartering with chickens or using shiny new trade currencies.

Final thought: Honestly, I'm not cheering for fiat 👤. With its manipulation and shady undertones, maybe it's high time we sought the truth beyond the illusion 🔍.

Enjoy diving deep into the true essence of wealth! 💰💥

"While fiat currency dances to the tune of governments, gold remains the steady rhythm of true wealth."

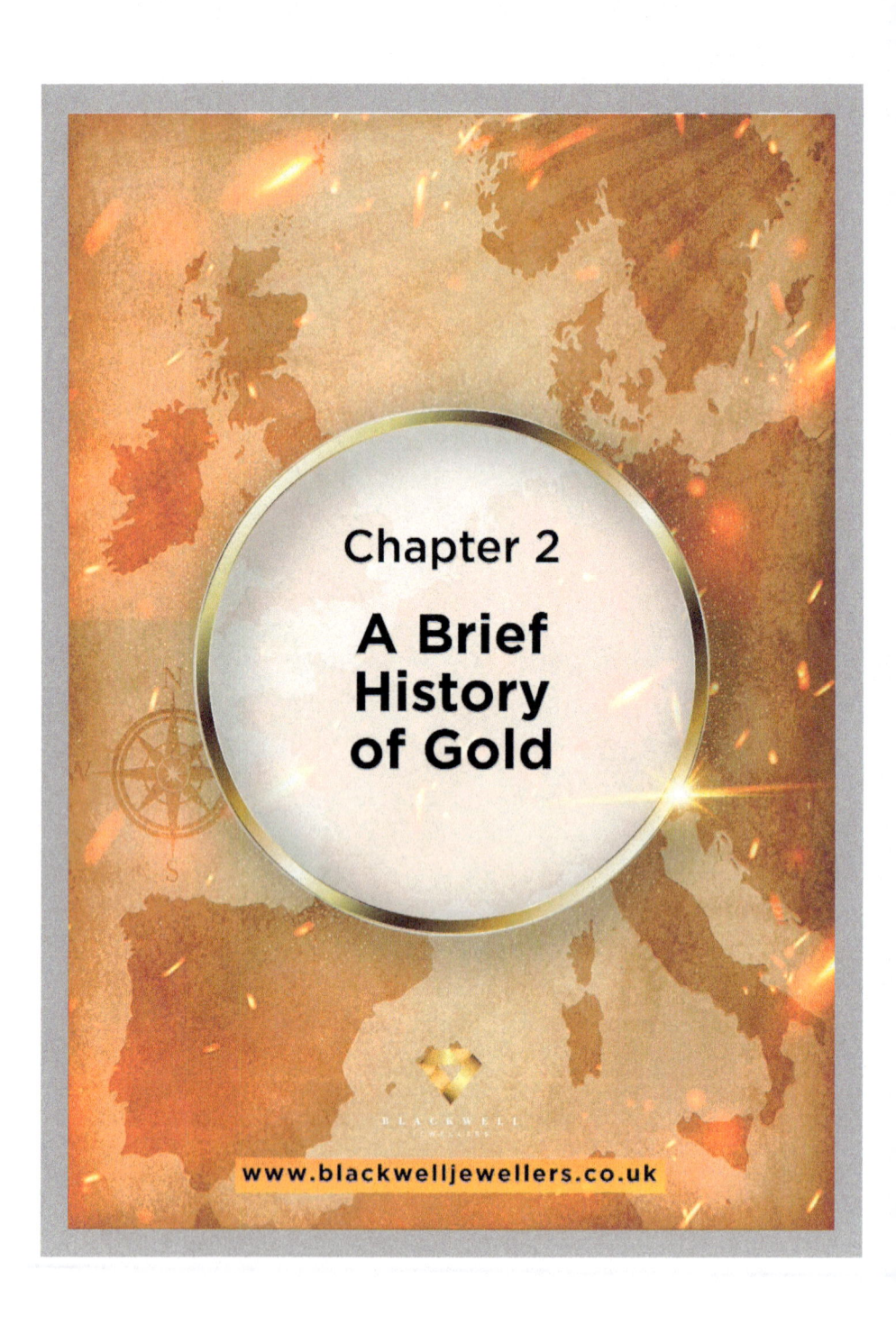

Chapter 2

A Brief History of Gold

www.blackwelljewellers.co.uk

"James's Fun Facts"

"Inflation alert!

When too much money gets printed, your quid buys less. Imagine going to the shop and suddenly, your favourite crisps are double the price.

Not on my watch!"

Chapter 2

A Brief History of Gold

For as long as humans have been on earth, gold has held a special We've quite a bit to unravel about gold here.

Now, as we traverse down the memory lane of human civilisation, it's almost impossible not to stumble upon the glittering tales of gold.

The lustrous metal has indeed been deeply intertwined with our history, shaping societies, economies, and values.

But why?

What makes gold so special, you ask?

Well, settle in, and let's embark on this riveting journey together.

Gold in Ancient Egypt

Our first stop is ancient Egypt, the cradle of civilisation. Picture the grandeur of the Pharaohs, and more likely than not, you'll find yourself imagining golden crowns, golden statues, and well, a lot of gold.

From as early as 3000 BC, Egyptians were mining this shiny treasure along the Nile.

They moulded it into exquisite jewellery, statues and other artifacts of significant cultural importance. In fact, gold was so influential that it also started being used as a form of currency around 2600 BC. Imagine buying a jug of wine with a gold ring, quite extraordinary, right?

Gold in Phoenician Culture

Next, we sail to the lands of the Phoenicians, the legendary seafaring folks. These chaps were incredibly fond of gold and went to great lengths (quite literally) to get their hands on it.

They established sprawling trade routes across the Mediterranean Sea and even took prisoners of war to toil in their gold mines. Not exactly the noblest way to procure gold, but it goes to show just how precious the metal was in their society.

Gold in Ancient Greece and Persia

Fast-forward a few centuries to around 600 BC, and we arrive in ancient Greece, where gold began to jingle in the pockets of many.

The Greeks were the pioneers of minting gold coins. Additionally, the Greeks adorned their gods and goddesses with gold, amplifying the divine allure.
Around the same time, the Persians too started adopting gold as a currency, setting a precedent for other civilisations to follow.

Gold in the Roman Empire

Jumping forward in time, we encounter Julius Caesar, a man with an insatiable appetite for conquest and, you guessed it, gold. As he conquered Europe around 56 BC, he filled Rome's coffers with enormous amounts of gold.

It's said that Rome's wealth was so substantial that it was hard to comprehend. But mind you, even such affluence couldn't save Rome from an eventual downfall, offering a stark reminder that all that glitters is not always... invincible.

Gold during the Dark Ages

Now, here's an era that certainly lived up to its name. The Dark Ages saw gold being hidden away, lost, or simply forgotten.

The once shining beacon of wealth and prosperity was shrouded in mystery and darkness. It took a while, roughly until 700 AD, for gold to regain its former glory and begin to glimmer brightly once again.

Gold in Medieval Europe

Alright, fast forward to Medieval Europe, and we find ourselves in the age of knights, castles, and a fair share of gold. In this era, you could often find gold clinking around in a merchant's purse or sparkling on a noble's attire.

But why was gold so prevalent?

Well, the answer is a bit more practical than you might think. You see, transporting large quantities of goods over long distances was quite the hassle.

Moreover, theft was a widespread issue. Gold, with its high value-to-weight ratio and non-corrosive properties, became the ideal solution. It could be transported easily and did not degrade over time. So, the merchants would often trade in gold, adding another significant chapter to the ongoing tale of our shiny friend.

Gold during the California Gold Rush

Now, let's move away from the gloomy castles of Europe and towards sunny California. Picture this: the year is 1848, and gold has just been discovered at Sutter's Mill.

What followed next was one of the most significant gold rushes in history, attracting hundreds of thousands of prospectors, all with dreams of striking it rich.

The sheer amount of gold unearthed during this period was so tremendous that it led to inflation. There was so much gold around that its value actually decreased temporarily.

Quite a twist, isn't it?

Gold in Modern Era

With the gold dust settling post the California gold rush, we move into the modern era. Today, gold is no longer jingling in our pockets or being traded at local markets.

Instead, you'll find most of it stored in large vaults by central banks or adorning people as jewellery.

Gold has come a long way from the Nile banks of Egypt to our present day. It has outlived empires, survived crises and still holds a revered place in our society.

But beyond its glimmering beauty, gold's allure also lies in its usefulness. It's highly conductive, resistant to tarnish, and excellent for making fine wires and thin sheets. Therefore, gold also finds significant application in electronics, dentistry, and even aerospace!

Introduction to the Impact of Financial Crises on Gold

From our deep dive into the history of gold so far, one thing is clear: gold is far more than a mere adornment. In times of financial upheaval, gold has consistently emerged as the knight in shining armour, or shall we say, the asset in shining armour.

The real question, though, is why?

What makes gold such a popular choice in times of financial trouble?

The answer lies in gold's stability. When traditional currencies falter and the stock market plummets, gold retains its value. It's considered a safe haven for investors during turbulent times. Let's delve into a few historical examples that illustrate this trend.

Tulip Mania (1637)

Let's kick things off with Tulip Mania. You heard it right, my friend! An actual mania around tulip bulbs in the 17th century.

The price of these beauties shot up to an astronomical 10 times the annual income of a skilled worker. However, like all bubbles, it burst, leaving many a Dutchman penniless.

The intriguing part?

The collapse in tulip prices caused an upswing in gold's value. Investors sold off their tulips and turned to gold, considered a more stable and valuable asset. So, in essence, when the tulip garden withered, gold, the resilient flower, stood tall.

Credit Crisis (1772)

The next pitstop on our tour of financial crises is the Credit Crisis of 1772. Following a period of rapid credit expansion, the bubble burst due to over-speculation and panic following rumours of a significant bank insolvency.

This crisis led to commercial bankruptcy, and the value of shares and other assets took a nosedive.

Guess what rose in response? Gold, of course. As the economic situation became more unstable, investors turned to the reliable glitter of gold for financial security, causing a significant upswing in its price.

Wall Street Crash (1929)

Fast forward to 1929 and we find ourselves in the midst of the Wall Street Crash.

This crisis marked the onset of the Great Depression, a period of extreme economic hardship in America. As the stock market crashed, guess which asset took centre stage?

You guessed it: our old friend, gold. People flocked to it as a safe haven, causing its price to increase significantly.

OAPEC Oil Crisis (1973)

In 1973, we saw the OAPEC Oil Crisis when the Organisation of Arab Petroleum Exporting Countries initiated an oil embargo. The embargo led to soaring oil prices and long fuel queues across America. As inflation increased, so did the price of gold. The golden rule prevailed yet again: when in crisis, turn to gold.

Global Financial Crisis (2007-2008)

Our last stop is the Global Financial Crisis of 2007-2008, the most significant economic disaster since the Great Depression.

Triggered by subprime mortgages and lack of regulatory oversight, this crisis saw countless people lose their jobs, homes, and savings.

Amid this grim scenario, gold emerged as a beacon of hope. As people rushed to this time-tested safe haven, gold prices climbed to unprecedented levels.

Learning from History: Financial Crisis, Government, and Individual Greed

When we dive headfirst into monetary history and cycles, it's akin to unravelling a well-kept secret. You see, there's a lot to learn, not just about the role of governments, but also the part we all play in creating these financial ebbs and flows.

Now, let's not get all huffy and puffy about it, but we must admit that it's easy to point a finger at the government for all our problems. Oh, the countless times we've all muttered, "Bloody government!" But take a step back, and you'll see that we're the ones who give them power. It's like a grand pantomime, and we're all part of the performance.

Moreover, history is littered with instances where, even without the government's assistance, people's greed has led to some daft decisions that wreaked havoc on our economy.

To put it bluntly, we don't need the government to cock up our economy. Given the right conditions, we humans do a pretty good job of it ourselves!

World War I: A Case Study

The Beginning of World War I and the Suspension of Gold Standard in Germany

For our final act, let's turn the clock back to World War I. The Germans decided to take a holiday from the gold standard and suspended the conversion of their currency (the mark) into gold and silver.

The war chest was replenished using the good old printing press, a dangerous tool if there ever was one.

The Treaty of Versailles and its Impact

Fast forward to 1919, when the Treaty of Versailles put a full stop to World War I. The treaty required Germany to make large reparation payments in gold marks.

The government, strapped for cash, started printing more marks. The result was an explosion in the money supply and a rapid increase in prices.

Hyperinflation and Collapse of the Mark

By 1923, the price levels in Germany had shot up, hitting levels that were once unfathomable. The government's price controls only worsened the situation. Businesses shied away from investing, not knowing their costs for the coming weeks or months, and workers demanded higher wages.

The situation spiralled out of control, culminating in hyperinflation and the collapse of the mark.

The Silver Lining: Gold's Immunity to Inflation

All this chaos did little to dampen the appeal of gold. Due to its limited supply and lack of a central authority controlling it, gold was immune to the inflationary pressures that brought Germany to its knees. Amidst the rubble, gold emerged, shining brighter than ever.

Impact on the Social Structure: The Rich, the Poor, and the Middle Class

The socio-economic impact of this crisis was devastating. The rich got richer, the poor remained poor, and the middle class?

They were almost wiped off the map. But as with all things in life, there were exceptions.

The Exception: Those Who Benefited from the Crisis

Despite the chaos, some individuals had the foresight or fortune to leverage the economic conditions to their advantage. They were the savvy investors, the risk-takers, those who knew the value of gold amidst a sea of worthless marks.

Conclusion

So, there you have it, from the ancient Egyptians to modern-day financial crises, we've journeyed through time to see how gold has always been more than just a shiny metal.

It's been a currency, a symbol of wealth, a saviour in tough times, and a beacon of stability in a world often plagued by financial chaos.

Whether you're an investor or a history buff, I hope our stroll through the annals of monetary history has left you with a greater appreciation for gold.

Remember, as Churchill once said, "The farther backward you can look, the farther forward you are likely to see."

So, keep an eye on the past, plan for the future, and always keep a nugget of gold close to hand.

James's Chapter Summary for the Busy Bee (Or a Quick Recap)

🌍 Gold Through the Ages: Humanity's bling-bling superstar!

EG Ancient Egypt: Pharaohs treated gold as credit cards circa 2600 BC.

🌊 Phoenicians: Oceanic gold miners and traders.

🏛 Ancient Greece & Persia: Introduced gold coins, the OG currency.

☐ Rome & Caesar: Gold frenzy! But even gold couldn't save Rome.

☺ Dark Ages: Gold played hide and seek till 700 AD.

⚔ Medieval Europe: Gold became a traveller's safeguard.

🙍 California Gold Rush: Gold overload decreased its value.

🏙 Modern Times: Gold in tech, dental, and space exploration.

💱 Gold During Financial Crises: The resilient superstar 😎.

🌷 Tulip Mania: Flowers failed; gold prevailed.

🏛 1772 Credit Crisis: Banking woes brought out gold's sparkle.

📉 1929 Wall Street Crash: Stocks tumbled; gold climbed.

⛽ 1973 OAPEC Oil Crisis: Oil's loss was gold's gain.

🌐 2007-2008 Global Crisis: Amidst turmoil, gold shone.

📚 History's Lessons: We all shape the economic story 🗨️. Personal and governmental greed impacts the tale.

🌍 World War I Deep Dive:

🇩🇪 Germany & Gold: Abandoning gold led to chaos.

📜 Treaty of Versailles: Germany's gold debts sped up hyperinflation.

🥇 Gold's Immunity: Inflation couldn't dull its shine.

👨‍👩 Social Impact: The rich thrived, the poor suffered, the middle dwindled. Gold savvies survived.

🔚 In Retrospect: Gold: The faithful ally across epochs. Churchill's wisdom? Study the past, plan the future, and keep a gold nugget close! ✨🥇🪙

"James's Fun Facts"

"Hold onto your monocles!

Printing more money without a backup plan?

It's kind of like counterfeiting. And we all know that's a naughty game.

"Inflation is the illusion of wealth; gold is the reality of it."

Chapter 3

The Birth of the Central Bank

www.blackwelljewellers.co.uk

"James's Fun Facts"

"Bit of a history trip:

The U.S. once made it illegal for citizens to hold onto their gold! 1933 was the year.

So, for a time, keeping gold was as rebellious as listening <u>to rock 'n' roll.</u>"

Chapter 3

The Birth of The Central Bank

Back in the 1300s, Europe was thriving with trade. Princes and traders used their own silver and gold coins, or other metallic coins, to buy and sell things. But there were some problems with this system.

Official coin prices were based on how much precious metal they contained, but the purity of these coins would frequently change. This made them not as valuable as you might have expected.

Another big problem was how difficult carrying bags of coins was, which also added more cost. And just imagine the headache when they needed to make international transactions!

This is when they needed to rely on European banks and families to transfer their debts into tradable deposit money.

This caused another problem: if one of these banks failed, it could take down the whole economy. A good example is when England's King Edward III couldn't repay his loans in the 14th century. Italy was hit hard by this because its economy was closely linked with England's.

In 1609, trade with the Baltic countries was flourishing. But clove importers wanted monetary reform; there were 14 mints in a very small area, all making their own coins, and this made it really hard to exchange them or to separate the good ones from the bad.

So after listening to the city of Amsterdam, the Bank of Amsterdam was founded. This bank provided deposit money to merchants, predominantly used for large transactions.

The bank wanted a 5% premium over metallic coin money. This became very popular, and off the back of this came other banks across the Netherlands.

But in 1672, the French, English and German armies attacked the Netherlands. After that, the banks weren't able to repay all their depositors. However, the Bank of Amsterdam was... It had enough coins to make payments.

The Dutch economy never fully recovered after the attack, but the Bank of Amsterdam became stronger than ever.

After a while, the bank changed a few policies. This meant no deposits could be redeemed for coins anymore, so all non-redeemable deposits were based on trust in the Bank of Amsterdam's authority.

Now keep in mind that this non-redeemable deposit money was still connected to the price of precious metals. People who accepted these deposits knew they could trade them in for metal coins if they needed to.

This turned out to be a good thing in 1763 when a merchant bank went bankrupt, sending shockwaves through Europe. But the Bank of Amsterdam stepped in as a lender and became the banker of the banking system.

But people only trusted this bank because it supposedly had a lot of gold coins. The bank had got too large for the city of Amsterdam to bail it out if there was a crisis. This happened when a war broke out and the city of Amsterdam started demanding more and more credit from the bank. People stopped trusting the bank, and it dissolved in 1819.

In 1688, England was invaded by the Dutch. William of Orange led his army to England, but this was more of an organised plan than an invasion. The British Army actually helped William overthrow the British monarchy, and William of Orange III became King William III.

It's funny, though, that this story has an ironic twist.

Many economists believe the invasion caused the creation of a central bank that would eventually take over the Bank of Amsterdam. This central bank allowed England to fight France in its Nine Years' War by transmitting funds to troops on the continent via Amsterdam.

But more importantly, it funded the war through the issue of banknotes. As we all know, wars are expensive, and this quickly turned excessive, which caused inflation.

In West India in 1793, a merchant got into trouble due to a war with France. They went to the Bank of England for support, which they got, but the Bank of England had a lot to deal with supporting the economy and the government while they were tied down by gold.

It's not surprising that the value of gold decreased when paper money became more common. The Bank of England had to stop people from exchanging gold for paper money in 1797, which lasted almost 25 years. So, the Bank of England, like the Bank of Amsterdam before it, started issuing paper money. This helped businesses during the early 19th century.

Central banks were introduced in Europe so everything would work well. The USA, which had a history of one banking crisis after another, also created their own version of a central bank. Even though central banking has a history of lying and crisis, and even supporting slave trade, it did seem to stabilise prices and finance. Everything was going well, until the 1950s, when high economy, economic growth, and inflation became the new norm.

But then in the 1990s and early 2000s, financial instability seemed to make a comeback. We'll talk about that later...

How the US Became the Global Gold Custodian: A Golden Tale

Picture this: The world had just emerged from the turbulent times of World War I. Cities lay in ruins, nations were financially depleted, and the global economy was in shambles.

But amidst this chaos, the US stood like a phoenix, its feathers gleaming gold - literally! By the time the war dust settled, Uncle Sam had amassed most of the world's gold reserves. You might wonder, "How on earth did that happen?"

It's a fascinating turn of events. During the war, European nations, with their economies stretched thin, turned to the US for loans.

And the US, being the generous financier, doled out loans not just in its own currency but also in gold. By the time the war was over, European vaults were echoing with emptiness when it came to gold, but their coffers were brimming with US dollars.

In the financial world, it was akin to trading in your shiny, precious golden necklace for a promise note.

But with great power (or gold, in this case) comes great responsibility.

The US needed a structure to handle this immense wealth and ensure the dollar's stability. Enter the Federal Reserve, the US's answer to a central bank. But here's the zesty twist: The Federal Reserve had the unique power to create currency out of thin air. Imagine having a magic printer that churns out legitimate money whenever you want!

Now, I know what you're thinking, "How can one just 'create' money without it being backed by anything?"

Good question!

The answer lies in the beauty of the reserve requirement system. The Federal Reserve was mandated to ensure that for every dollar they brought into existence, a certain portion had to be backed by gold.

The Federal Reserve Act of 1913 was pretty specific about it: 40% of every dollar had to be backed either by gold or another tangible currency.

It was like a tightrope act, balancing faith in the dollar with the actual gold in the vaults.

And for a while, this magic act worked wonders. The dollar was the rockstar of currencies. However, as with all great rockstars, there was a period of doubt and downfall.

The Great Depression hit, and with it came dwindling confidence in the dollar. Suddenly, everyone wanted to trade their paper money for gold. The demand for the dollar overseas plummeted faster than a lead balloon.

In this atmosphere of economic panic, President Franklin D. Roosevelt took centre stage. Declaring a national emergency in 1933, he played a card no one saw coming:

He banned the private ownership of gold. Imagine waking up one day and being told, "Sorry, you can't have that shiny thing anymore." And as if that wasn't shocking enough, the next year he changed the price tag on gold, hiking it from $20.67 an ounce to $35.

And just to make sure everyone was on board with this new gold-less vision, all privately held gold was rounded up, with the government ensuring compliance with a rather persuasive argument - the barrel of a gun.

And so, in a series of bold, unprecedented moves, the US not only took control of the world's gold supply but also set the stage for a new era of financial systems and currency dynamics.

An era where paper promises would often overshadow tangible wealth. Quite the golden adventure, don't you think?

The Real Reason Franklin D. Roosevelt Outlawed Gold

Look, let's dive deeper into this fascinating chapter of American history, a time when Uncle Sam said, "No more gold for you!"

Imagine, one day, waking up and the government telling you, "Hey, that gold you've been keeping in your safe? Hand it over." That's basically what happened in 1933.

President Franklin D. Roosevelt, in a move that probably had a few jaws dropping, banned the private ownership of gold. Now, I know what you're thinking: "Why on earth would he do that?" Hang tight, we're getting there.

But first, let's address the elephant in the room. Many folks were yelling, "That's unconstitutional!" And it wasn't just your average Joe; legal experts, economists, and politicians were divided on this issue. There was a significant hullabaloo, to say the least.

So, diving into the 'why' – just days before Roosevelt pulled this wild card, Congress had passed the Emergency Banking Act. Nestled within its pages was a seemingly innocent provision.

This little clause gave the Federal Reserve the green light to churn out $1.5 billion in 'notes' to help the struggling nation. Think of these notes as IOUs, a promise from the Federal Reserve to the US Treasury.

It's like if you told your friend, "I don't have the money now, but I promise I'll pay you back," but on a much, much larger scale.

But, and here's the tricky part, for the Fed's IOUs to be legit, they had to be backed by something tangible, something real.

And what's more real than gold?

There was just one teeny, tiny hiccup: the Federal Reserve was a bit short on the shiny stuff.

Enter Roosevelt with a solution that was as audacious as it was desperate. His executive order was a clarion call for all private citizens to hand over their gold.

Essentially, Roosevelt was telling everyone, "Give us your gold, so we can keep our promise." This move turned personal gold stashes into the backbone of the Federal Reserve's notes.

And here's where it gets juicy: while on the surface, it looked like an attempt to stabilize the nation's economy (and to some extent, it was), it was also a sneaky way to rescue the Federal Reserve.

It's kind of like helping out a friend in need, but then realizing that friend is actually a distant cousin to the government.

To top it all off, this entire scenario painted the Federal Reserve in a rather peculiar light. It was supposed to be this big, official institution, right?

Yet here it was, reliant on everyday people to bail it out. This bold move by Roosevelt underscored a critical point: the Federal Reserve might wear government colours, but at its core, it's its own beast, dancing to its own tune and accountable to, well, seemingly no one.

What is Fractional Reserve Banking?

Ever found yourself daydreaming, not about sandy beaches or that next big vacation, but about where your money actually comes from?

A tad unusual, I admit. I'm not talking about the pay check or that side gig you're hustling on. I mean the grand system, the invisible machinery that churns out those numbers in your bank account.

Sounds like something right out of an epic saga, doesn't it? Let's journey through the world of fractional reserve banking together.

Picture this: you walk into your local bank, the one with actual doors and windows. As you deposit your hard-earned money, you might imagine it tucked away in a vault reminiscent of scenes from heist movies.

Mountains of gold, bundles of cash neatly tied... But here's the twist: banks in our world have a slightly different game plan.

Enter the idea of 'fractional reserve'. While 'fractional' means a part of the whole, 'reserve' is what's kept aside for later. In banking, this translates to holding back just a "fraction" of the total deposits.

If we're making a rough estimate, it's about 10%. You might be thinking, "Why only a teeny-tiny slice?"

Because the rest? Well, it's out there spinning the wheels of our economy.

Your money, particularly the 90% that's not lounging around in the vault, is busy. It's in Mr. Partridges new car.

It's in the shiny oven Ms. Smith just installed in her bakery. And here's where it gets intriguing: the journey of that money doesn't end there.

When Ms. smith pays her supplier, that money likely finds its way back into a bank.

And then?

A repeat performance!

The bank retains a fraction and lends the rest. It's a continuous dance of deposit-lend-spend-deposit, magnifying the original sum's impact on the economy.

Mind = blown!

But hold up. "Isn't this a precarious dance?" you may ask. Spot on! Banking, in this model, is an art of balance. Banks need to ensure they can cover everyday withdrawals while also profiting from loan interests.

Picture it as a ballet on a high wire, albeit with safety nets underneath.

And here's the crucial part: this system, while brilliant in fuelling economic growth, is not without its risks.

If too many bad loans are made or if too many people rush to withdraw their money simultaneously, things can get shaky.

It's a game of trust, and when that trust wavers (think economic crises), banks can find themselves in hot water.

So, why should you care?

Because this very mechanism propels our modern economy. It backs investments, bolsters businesses, and paves the way for consumer spending. Moreover, being savvy about this gives you a lens into the broader economic rhythm.

In essence, fractional reserve banking isn't just some by-the-book procedure. It's the pulse of contemporary finance, underpinning countless success stories and personal endeavours. It's a testament to the vibrant, dynamic life of money.

The next time you check your bank balance or walk past your local bank, remember there's an intricate ballet unfolding behind those numbers.

And just like that, you've unlocked another layer of the complex, enthralling world of finance. Who knew the inner workings of banking could be this captivating?

Why Should Gold Investors Care?

Remember those mega house parties back in the day, where the hosts, trying to keep the vibe alive, invited more and more people until the floorboards creaked and the next-door neighbours plotted revenge?

Only here, instead *Well, fractional reserve banking isn't too dissimilar from those parties.*

of people, its money being shuffled about. And much like those party planners, gold investors are always thinking two steps ahead.

Now, I might've been a tad dramatic comparing fractional reserve banking to a Ponzi scheme, but there's a hint of truth there.

Just like a party can't fit unlimited guests, the system can't infinitely create money without consequences.

The bank is dancing a delicate waltz, hoping enough folks don't simultaneously dash to pull out their cash. And if they do, well... it's akin to that moment the music stops, and the police show up.

But where does gold come into this disco?

Picture gold as that VIP guest everyone respects—the celebrity presence that never goes out of style, doesn't need too much hype, and simply holds their ground.

As the wild dance of fractional reserve banking whirls on, gold calmly sips its drink, unaffected by the frenzy.

Gold investors, my friend, are a bit like party planners with a secret stash of A-lister contacts. They know the value of having that superstar guest.

When everything else is in disarray—perhaps too many people were invited, or the snacks run out—there's still that one element that keeps the party's prestige high.

Why is that?

Because gold, unlike other assets, isn't intertwined with the gyrations of fractional reserve banking. When banks are in turmoil and confidence dwindles, gold retains, and sometimes even elevates, its value.

It's a glimmering anchor in an otherwise stormy sea. Think of it as that lifeboat on a luxury cruise—most of the time, you're just enjoying the onboard entertainment, but if things go south, you'd be darn thankful it's there.

Still, fractional reserve banking isn't just a reckless teenager throwing a wild bash. It's a complex, often misunderstood, marvel of modern economics.

It powers investment, fuels dreams, and keeps economies humming. But like anything powerful, it needs to be managed wisely. Because if it goes off the rails, it can bring the entire economic household down with it.

And that's the moment gold investors have been prepping for. While others scurry in panic, these smart cookies, with their golden treasures, are ready.

It's like having an umbrella on a cloudy day; maybe it won't rain, but if it does, you're not getting wet.

In essence, it's about security, foresight, and a dash of wisdom. In a world of financial acrobatics, gold remains steadfast and unflappable. As currencies wobble and economies shake, the golden allure endures.

So next time you hear of gold investors, imagine them as savvy party planners, always ready, always a step ahead.

And if you ever consider joining their ranks, remember, while it's grand to dance to the beats of the global economy, it's equally wise to have that timeless VIP guest—gold—in your corner.

Because as history has shown, when the music fades and the crowd disperse, gold remains, shining as ever.

James's Chapter Summary for the Busy Bee (Or a Quick Recap)

🏦: **Birth of Central Banking** - The inception of centralized monetary control in response to European trade complexities.

🌍🪙: **European Trade Quandaries -** Europe's thriving trade faced obstacles due to inconsistent coin purity.

💼🔥: **Banking's Precariousness** - The European banking system's fragility threatened economies, accentuated by royal defaults.

NL 🔄 GB: **Amsterdam to England** - From the Bank of Amsterdam's innovative solutions to the Bank of England's establishment, central banking took root.

💷🖨: **Paper Money Evolution** - The Bank of England shifted from gold to paper money, influencing Europe and the USA.

📈🪙: **20th Century Banking Rollercoaster** - Central banks offered financial stability, but the late century brought turbulence.

🌍🏆: **US: Gold's New Home** - Post-WWI dynamics turned the US into the world's primary gold reservoir.

📜🚫💥: **Roosevelt's Bold Move** - The Great Depression prompted President Roosevelt to ban private gold ownership.

💬 💵 ❓: **Dive into Fractional Reserve Banking** - A look at how banks lend more than they hold and its implications.

🏢 🎉 💥: **Banking & Gold's Tandem** - The delicate balance between the ever-evolving banking system and the stable allure of gold.

Chapter 4
The National Debt is Soaring!

www.blackwelljewellers.co.uk

"James's Fun Facts"

"This might ruffle some feathers:

Central banks might look solid, but there have been times when they've caused financial panics by manipulating gold reserves.

Oops!"

Chapter 4

The National Debt is Soaring!

Pop quiz! What can soar higher than an eagle, balloon faster than you can say "Wait, what?" and gives economists more than just a mild headache? If you said the national debt, ding ding ding!

You've hit the jackpot!

Let's rewind a bit and head over to the glitzy world of the United States. America, with its vast landscapes, iconic landmarks, and Hollywood shine, also has another claim to fame — its ever-mounting national debt. And boy, is it a rollercoaster!

Picture this: it's a sunny day on March 16th, 2007. The birds are chirping, Wall Street's bustling, and Congress is in session. With a shuffle of papers and some firm nods, they make a move.

The national debt ceiling, that imaginary line we're not supposed to cross, gets a little lift from $8.2 trillion to a whopping $9 trillion.

But here's the kicker: a blink later, that debt almost touches the newly raised ceiling, cruising to $8.98 trillion.

You'd think someone might hit the brakes, right? But no! With the bravado of a daredevil, Congress gives the green light for the fifth hike, pushing our dizzying ceiling to $9.8 trillion.

Imagine hosting a party and repeatedly moving the "Do Not Cross" tape further back because your guests just can't resist dancing past the line!

Fast forward to the present, and as I pen this down, rumour has it that America's national debt could be doing the cha-cha past $24 trillion by the end of 2022. That's not just a jump; it's a moonwalk!

But let's pivot to the real golden question here: why should the sparkle-eyed gold enthusiasts care?

Here's the scoop: as the national debt skyrockets, the allure of gold grows stronger. This isn't just any regular see-saw; it's a teeter-totter of global financial implications.

A higher national debt makes currencies wobbly, economies unsure, and investors jittery. But gold? It struts forward, head held high, shimmering brighter than ever.

In essence, as Uncle Sam's tab grows, those who've bet on gold might just be chuckling their way to the bank (or the gold vault).

So, if you've got a soft spot for this shiny metal, you're in for quite the thrilling journey! Buckle up, and let's delve deeper into this golden dance of debt.

The Return of Sound Money

Alright, let's dive into the maze of sound money. Imagine your kitchen faucet. Now, picture it pouring out water non-stop, flooding your kitchen.

That water?

It's somewhat akin to the endless money being printed by governments. It's as if someone accidentally leaned on the 'print' button and forgot to lift off.

And this isn't just a quirky printer error; it has real-world ramifications. The main one? Our old nemesis, inflation.

You know inflation, right? It's the sneaky villain that makes everything more expensive. Remember when you could grab a quality coffee for just a couple of bucks?

Well, thanks to inflation, that same coffee now probably costs way more, even though it's the exact same brew.

The logic is straightforward: the more money we have in circulation (thanks to those tireless printing presses), the less each dollar is worth.

It's like if you had a limited-edition toy; it's valuable because there aren't many around. But if suddenly everyone had that toy, it wouldn't be as special anymore, right?

And so, as the value of our money drops, things get pricier. Now, central banks, seeing this mess unfold, try a trick: they keep interest rates low.

Why?

Because they hope it'll encourage people to spend and invest rather than hoarding money in assets like, you guessed it, gold.

However, here's the twist. The ever-pumping money machine can't go on forever. At some point, the sheer volume of newly minted money will lead to intense inflationary pressures.

It's like blowing air into a balloon; eventually, it's going to pop.

When this bubble looks ready to burst, central banks have no choice but to raise interest rates. Why? They hope this move will control the runaway inflation. But there's a side effect.

As interest rates go up, traditional investments like bonds lose their shine. They're not the attractive, steady options they once were.

And where do people often turn when looking for a stable investment during rocky times?

Bingo! It's our shiny friend, gold. Gold becomes the lifeboat in this financial storm, offering a refuge from the wavering values of fiat currencies.

The narrative is clear: when money loses its sheen, gold starts to gleam. It's the financial world's poetic justice. And for those savvy enough to see the signs, gold doesn't just offer protection; it presents opportunity. So, as we navigate these turbulent monetary waters, maybe it's time to ask: Are we ready for the return of sound money?

The Weakening of America's Global Dominance

Imagine a world where one nation holds the steering wheel, guiding the course of global affairs, both politically and economically.

That's been America for the better part of the last century. From Hollywood movies to Wall Street, the U.S. imprint on the world has been undeniable. However, things are never static in the realm of international relations.

Recently, the spotlight on the global stage has been growing wider, accommodating more players. America's starring role is shifting to more of an ensemble cast.

The world isn't just watching Hollywood anymore; they're also tuned into Bollywood, Nollywood, and other burgeoning industries. Financially, Wall Street isn't the only bustling financial hub – think Shanghai, Tokyo, or London.

Now, here's the interesting bit for investors: As America's relative position ebbs, there's a ripple effect on the global trust in the U.S. dollar. Investors from Tokyo to Toronto begin pondering, "If the U.S. isn't the sole power player anymore, should all my assets be tied up in dollars?"

It's like betting all your chips on one number in a game of roulette when the wheel is increasingly unpredictable.

And that's where gold waltzes in, like a timeless classic at a modern dance party. Gold doesn't pledge allegiance to any single flag.

It doesn't care about geopolitics or the rise and fall of superpowers. It's been a symbol of wealth and stability long before the U.S. dollar became the world's reserve currency, and it'll likely remain one long after.

So, as international investors contemplate a world where the U.S. isn't the only major influencer, they're looking for safer, more universally trusted places to park their wealth.

Enter gold. As more and more investors diversify their portfolios, moving away from dollar-centric assets, gold's allure only strengthens.

This isn't about a decline in America's greatness, but rather a reflection of a multipolar world, where power and influence are more dispersed.

And in such a world, assets that stand independent of any one nation's trajectory, like gold, become even more valuable.

For those with an eye on the horizon, understanding these global shifts can be the key to safeguarding and even growing wealth.

So, while the future might be a tad unpredictable, some things, like the enduring appeal of gold, remain brilliantly consistent.

The Decline of Trust in Institutions

It's the 1970s. Disco rules the airwaves, bell-bottoms are the height of fashion, and there's a growing unease in the air. It's not just the questionable fashion choices.

Trust in big institutions – governments, major corporations, and those all-important banks – starts to wobble.

Now, fast forward a bit. 2008. The world of finance is in chaos. Banks, which once stood as pillars of stability, are suddenly on shaky ground. Bailouts, government interventions – it's all very messy.

And guess what? Trust in these giants takes a major nosedive. People start giving their banks the side-eye, wondering, "Can I really rely on you?"

It's not just about the financial side of things. It's deeper than that. It's about trust. If we can't trust the big institutions to have our backs, where do we turn?

Enter stage right: assets that have seen empires rise and fall, yet remained solid. I'm talking about gold.

Gold isn't just some shiny rock we love for its sparkle. It's a beacon of consistency in an ever-changing financial landscape. It's not governed by a singular entity or subject to the whims of a particular government's monetary policy.

Gold is...well, gold. It's been valuable since the days of ancient civilizations and remains so today.

And here's the kicker: As trust in traditional systems dwindles and national debts rise (yes, they're still skyrocketing), the allure of gold shines brighter.

Think about it. We've got big-ticket programs like Social Security and Medicare. Wonderful in theory, but they come with a price tag—a price tag we haven't fully covered.

These are commitments, promises made to people. And promises need to be kept.

Now, we could see taxes skyrocket in an attempt to foot the bill for these programs. Or there could be other financial manoeuvres made to try and balance the books. But through all these potential economic rollercoasters, there's one asset that remains steadfast: gold.

So, for those looking to anchor their wealth in something tangible, something that's seen the world change and yet remained a beacon of value, gold is it.

It's like the trusty ship in a stormy sea of financial uncertainty. And as the waves get choppier, more and more investors are hopping aboard, hoping to sail through the turmoil unscathed.

So, if you've got a soft spot for gold, it's not just about the glint or the weight of it in your hand. It's about stability, history, and a touch of rebellion against the uncertainty of modern finance. To all the gold aficionados out there, now's your time to shine!

The International IOU: Why Most the World's Currency Reserves are Bonds, Not Cash

Alright, let's dive into this wild world of finance, which sometimes feels like a crazy board game, but with way more zeros at the end.

Ever wondered how countries deal with their massive stacks of money?

Spoiler: They aren't tossing wads of cash back and forth like in a rap video. The reality?

It's kinda like a high-stakes game of Monopoly, just way more complex.

So, here's the thing: Money isn't always about those crisp notes or coins you have in your pocket. On the big world stage, the major players—yeah, I'm talking about those big central banks—aren't mainly dealing with cash.

Nope. They're more into something called bonds. Think of bonds like fancy IOUs; basically, promises that they'll pay back later.

Now, these US Treasury bonds? They're like the VIP tickets everyone wants to snag.

They're kinda famous for being reliable. It's like when that popular influencer endorses a product, and suddenly everyone wants it.

That's these bonds for central banks.

Here's where things get interesting. When a country needs more money, they don't just magically print it. They sell a bond (a.k.a. that IOU) to their bank.

The bank then says, "Alright, cool. Here's some money for that promise." But get this: that money isn't based on actual gold or cash somewhere. It's kind of like getting a gift card but not being totally sure if there's money loaded on it.

Breaking it down: The government gives an IOU (the bond) to the bank. The bank gives them currency (money) in return. This new money will be used later to buy back that bond. It's like saying, "I owe you," getting something for it, and then later paying back what you owe. It's like a loop of promises.

Now, among all these promises flying around, there's one thing that doesn't waver, doesn't change, and doesn't need anyone vouching for it.

That's gold. Unlike these promises or IOUs, gold has been, well, gold for ages. It's solid, it's real, and it doesn't rely on someone's promise to have value.

So, for anyone keen on gold, remember: In this wild game of financial promises and IOUs, gold is like that rare, unbeatable card you want in your hand. It's the real deal. And trust me, this story only gets juicier. Stay tuned!

Why Does This Matter? The Reason Gold is Still Important in Today's Economy

The reason this matters is because it means most of the world's currency is actually debt. And as we all know, debt isn't a sustainable situation.

For debt to be sustainable, there needs to be continuous economic growth so more money can be generated to pay off debts. But what happens when economic growth slows down or stops entirely?

That's when debt begins to weigh down on an economy and can eventually lead to financial collapse.

So what does this have to do with gold?

Well, historically speaking, gold has been one of the most stable forms of wealth. It doesn't corrode or tarnish over time, and it's not affected by inflation like fiat currencies are.

That's why central banks typically hold a certain percentage of their reserves in gold—because it provides stability and security in times of economic uncertainty.

The international IOU system may seem confusing at first, but it's actually quite simple once you understand how it works. And understanding how it works is relevant because it helps us understand why gold is still such an important part of today's economy.

The Bond Market Is Crazy!

If you follow the bond market at all, you'll know it's been on a wild ride lately. Interest rates have been all over the place, and there's a lot of uncertainty about what's going to happen next.

But did you know the bond market is kind of a mess too? I'm not just talking about the recent volatility either. I'm talking about the fundamental way bonds work. Allow me to explain...

When you buy a bond, you're lending money to a government or corporation. In return, they promise to pay you interest for a set period of time, and return your principal at the end of the term.

That's all well and good, but there's a little bit of a problem. You see, when the government or corporation goes to redeem the bond, they don't actually have the money. They just have an IOU.

Now normally this wouldn't be a problem. They could just go out and borrow the money from someone else, and then pay you back with interest. But what if nobody will lend them money?

That's where things start to get really crazy.

As explained previously, to create currency, the government sells a bond to their central bank, the central bank writes a cheque and buys the bond.
The currency now exists, and can be used to redeem the bond later. So now we have a situation where the currency is an IOU for the bond, and the bond is an IOU for the currency!

It's like one big circle of debt nobody can escape from.

The bond market is definitely in a state of flux right now. But even if interest rates stabilise and everything goes back to normal, we're still left with a system that's fundamentally broken. The next time there's a financial crisis, who knows what could happen?

We might end up with even more worthless paper IOUs circulating around! If you want to protect your wealth, buying gold is still your best bet. It might not earn interest like bonds do, but at least you KNOW it'll hold its value. The banks just make stuff up.

Basically, the government pumps cash into the system by paying people and buying stuff with the currency, then people deposit that currency into banks.

The banks end up with lots of currency. And when someone wants to buy a house, they take out a loan from the bank by signing a mortgage.

But here's the thing: the mortgage says 'IOU X-amount of currency, plus X-amount of interest'. So, the bank creates a book entry for the amount of currency you borrowed, and at the same time, they create a book entry as a debt you owe on your loan account. On the bank's balance sheet, liabilities are netted out against assets, and everything stays balanced.

But wait just one second!

The bank didn't loan you any of their actual physical currency they had on hand. They just created some book entries. So basically, the government is just making stuff up and calling it money.

The government is making money out of thin air and calling it legal tender. If that doesn't sound fishy to you, then I don't know what does.

In my opinion, we should all be using gold as our primary currency. Gold can't be created out of thin air like paper money can; it's a finite resource that has value because we all agree it does.

That's why gold has been used as a form of money for thousands of years. So next time you're thinking about saving up for a rainy day, consider buying some gold instead of putting your money in the bank.

You might be surprised at how much more valuable it is in the long run!

The Derivatives Monster

Alright, keep reading, because we're about to embark on a wild ride through the dazzling world of derivatives!

Let's start with a story: The Mortgage-Backed Mayhem. Picture it: a super cool tool in finance called the mortgage-backed security.

Sounds fancy, right?

Well, it got a bit too fancy and played a starring role in what we call the subprime mortgage mess.

Think of a movie scene where the star makes a huge mistake— only, this was a real-life blockbuster gone wrong.

Why did this mess happen?

One word: temptation.

The Bank of England let its interest rates chill at record lows for a really long time.

This caused a tidal wave of money-making and credit-creating action.

It's like throwing a massive sale at your favourite store and everyone goes nuts, buying everything in sight!

And, of course, our dear sterling (the currency, not the silver) felt the pinch and lost some of its shine, making house prices skyrocket.

Banks, meanwhile, had a party of their own. They played a bit fast and loose, giving out house loans like free candy at a parade.

The problem?

Some folks got houses way beyond their means. Picture it like being handed the keys to a spaceship when you can't even drive a car!

Then, feeling like they hit the jackpot, these same folks started treating their homes like personal cash machines, splurging on stuff like the latest tech toys and flashy rides.

Now, the sting in the tale: subprime mortgages. When someone couldn't pay back, it wasn't just their money going down the drain.

The bank lost out too - both the money and the house! And remember those mortgage-backed securities?

They're like bundles of mortgages all packaged together.

If many people can't pay up, it's like a domino effect, causing chaos all around.

Remember 2008?

Yep, that's when a big bank named Lehman Brothers tripped and caused a global financial earthquake. That's the subprime mess in action!

But wait! What in the world are Derivatives?

Picture derivatives as these chameleons in the financial jungle. Their value changes based on the value of something else – be it stocks, bonds, or even our shiny friend, gold.

Mortgage-backed securities?

Just one species of this chameleon. It's like having a card that can change its powers based on the cards around it in a game.

Derivatives can be a gamble. If you're feeling lucky and think, say, gold prices will soar, you might bet on a gold derivative, hoping to make some serious coin if you're right.

Trading these chameleons can happen in two arenas: exchanges, where there are rules and referees like the SEC keeping an eye on things, and the wilder lands of Over-the-Counter (OTC) where it's a bit more... freestyle.

So, there you have it! Derivatives: the mysterious shapeshifters of the financial realm, both enchanting and enigmatic. And always, always worth keeping an eye on!

Why Are Derivatives Dangerous?

The vast majority of derivatives are created OTC, through private agreements instead of traded through an exchange.

This lack of regulation means there's no central authority overseeing the derivative market.

As a result, derivatives can be extremely risky because there's no way to know for sure what might happen with them.

Another reason derivatives are so dangerous is because they're often highly leveraged. Leverage is when you use borrowed money to increase your potential return on investment.

 For example, if you have £100 and borrow £99 so you can buy £199 worth of shares in a stock, you're using leverage.

The problem with leverage is that it also amplifies your losses.

So, if the stock price goes down instead of up, you not only lose your original £100 investment, but you also have to pay back the £99 you borrowed.

This can quickly lead to bankruptcies for both individuals and corporations alike. One final reason derivatives are dangerous is because they're often complex financial instruments even experts don't fully understand.

For example, collateralised debt obligations (CDOs) are a type of derivative made up of bundles of loans ranging from mortgages to credit card debt.

CDOs were at least partially responsible for causing the 2008 financial crisis because even the people who created them didn't really understand how they worked!

The derivatives monster is a big, scary beast made up of all different kinds of derivatives, and it's a menace to the world's financial system.

So remember: next time someone offers you a derivative investment opportunity, think twice before taking them up on it!

James's Chapter Summary for the Busy Bee (Or a Quick Recap)

"The National Debt is Soaring!"

🏃📈: U.S. debt rises, causing widespread concern.

📅📊: Debt ceiling continuously adjusted.

🌍💵: Rising debt enhances gold's allure.

"The Return of Sound Money"

🖨️💵: Excessive money printing threatens stability.

🍥📈: Inflation reduces purchasing power.

📉🌟: Gold stands as a monetary anchor.

"The Weakening of America's Global Dominance"

🌍🛡️: Evolving global power dynamics.

💱🔄: Shift from dollar assets boosts gold.

💥🌍: Gold's consistent global value.

"Trust in Institutions Declines"

🏛️📉: Falling trust in major institutions.

😟🏢: Banks symbolize increasing uncertainty.

💥🛡️: Gold remains a reliable asset.

"Gold's Modern Importance"

🌍📉: Economic growth struggles to counteract debt.

🔺🏢: Gold provides a stable contrast to fiat currencies.

💰📜: Gold's significance in the global IOU system.

"Bond Market Unpredictability"

📈💵: The bond market's erratic behaviour.

🔄🔗: Complex debt cycle with bonds.

"Derivative Risks"

🎬🏠: Risky mortgage-backed securities.

📉2008: Financial collapse epitomized by Lehman.

🚫👮: Unregulated derivative trading.

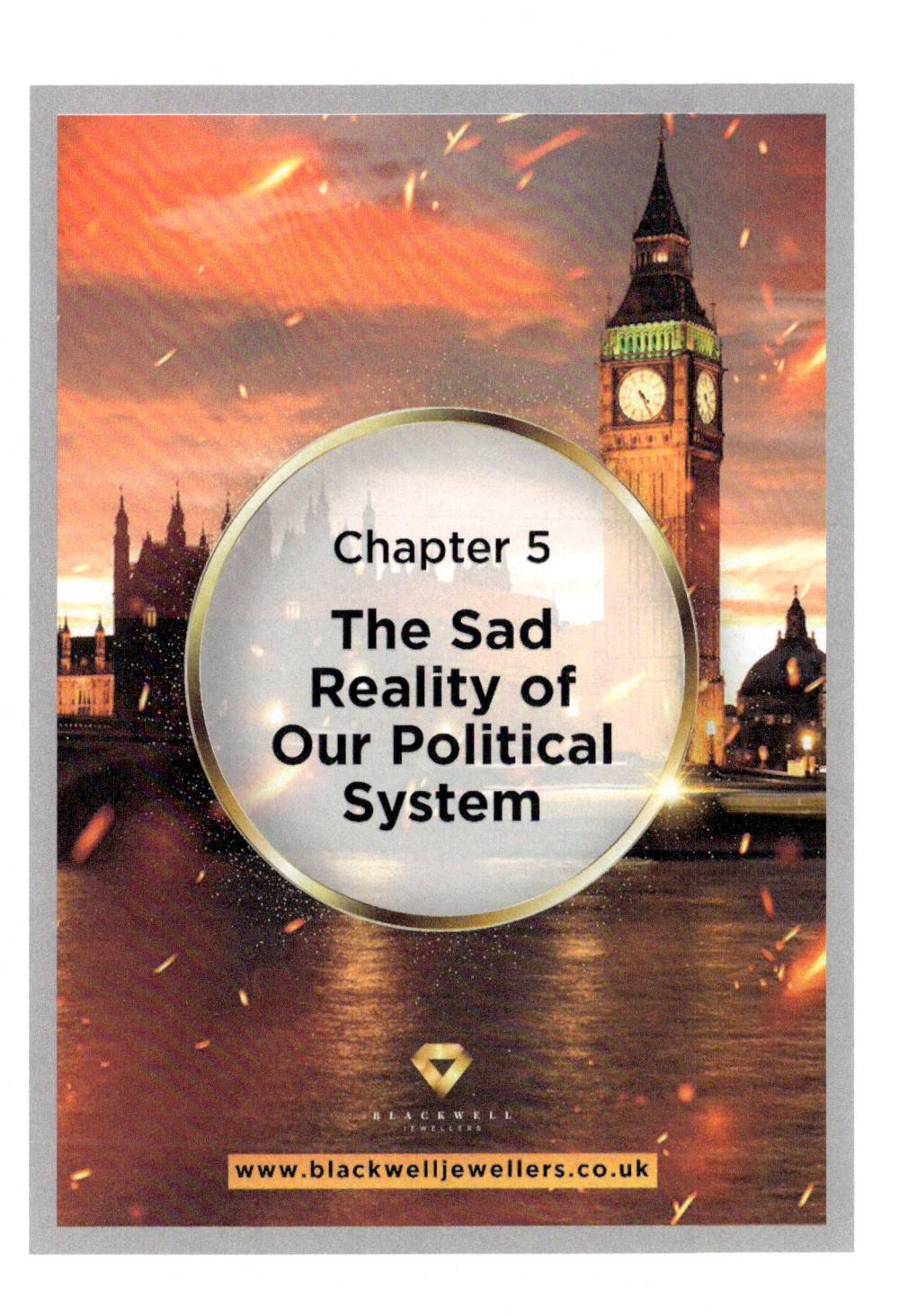

Chapter 5

The Sad Reality of Our Political System

"James's Fun Facts"

"If you've ever felt heavy-hearted?

It could be the gold!

The human body contains about 0.2 milligrams of gold, mostly in our blood.

No wonder we've got such golden personalities!"

Chapter 5

The Sad Reality of Our Political System

I'm sure you're all familiar with the old saying, "There's no such thing as a free lunch." Well, it turns out there's also no such thing as 'free' from the government.

Sure, politicians may promise to give you free this or free that, but they never tell you where the money for all that 'free stuff' is going to come from. In reality, it's coming out of your pocket.

Politicians are always promising more and more free stuff. But what they don't tell us is that nothing is really free. Someone has to pay for it eventually, and that someone is usually the taxpayer.

It may be nice to get a little something for nothing, but the truth is that our political system makes it very difficult for politicians to plan for anything more than four years in the future.

The only way a politician can get elected is by promising to give out more free stuff than the other person running against them. But the public doesn't realise it isn't really free.

If a politician suggests we should cut back on any area of the budget, they'll be looked down upon and people will think badly of them.

This is because every issue is seen as the most important issue of our time, and no one wants to make the tough decisions that need to be made in order to improve our economy.

The government should stay out of our business!

The Problem with Promises

Whenever there's a problem, people always say the same thing: "The government should do something about it." They all seem to think the government should be responsible for solving everyone's problems.

For example, when major companies get into financial trouble, they think the government should bail them out. Or when homeowners can't afford their mortgage payments, they think the government should save them.

But we don't seem to make the connection that whenever the government 'does something about it', it's usually less efficient and more expensive than if the private sector did it, and the public has to pay for it through taxes or inflation. So in the end, our pockets are getting hit.

The Government's Role

The government's role is to protect us from harm and to provide for our common defence. That's it!

It's not the government's job to bail out businesses nor to save people from foreclosure. The private sector can do that much better and at a fraction of the cost.

And when the government does get involved, it often makes things worse. Just look at the current financial crisis.

The government has been bailing out banks and businesses left and right, but has anyone seen any improvement? The economy is still struggling.

We need to start demanding that our elected officials stop wasting our money on bailouts and other unnecessary programmes. We need to hold them accountable for their actions and vote them out if they don't listen to us. We also need to support businesses that are run efficiently and provide good value for our money. Only by doing these things can we hope to get our economy back on track.

So next time you hear someone say the government should do something about a problem, just remember it's usually better if they stay out of it!

We as citizens need to take responsibility for ourselves and our businesses and not rely on the government to bail us out every time something goes wrong. Otherwise, we'll all end up paying for it in the end.

Big Government is Bad for Business

It's no secret that big government is a problem in the UK. The government is so large and bloated that it's sucking up more and more of the country's resources.

This is bad news for businesses because it means there's less money to go around. And when there's less money to go around, businesses suffer, and inflation goes up.

There are a few dangers that come with having such a large government. First, it's very expensive to maintain. The government has to pay for the salaries of all its employees, as well as their benefits and pensions.

All this costs taxpayers billions of pounds every year.

Second, big government can be very inefficient. There are so many layers of bureaucracy that it can be difficult to get anything done.

This can lead to waste and inefficiency, which end up costing taxpayers even more money.

Finally, big government can be very intrusive. The government has its hands in all sorts of things, from healthcare to education to welfare. This can lead to a loss of freedom and liberty for citizens.

This is a recipe for disaster. When government gets too big, it crowds out private enterprise and stifles innovation. This leads to higher prices and less economic growth. That's why gold is such a valuable investment; it's a hedge against inflation.

The Benefits of Gold Investing

Gold is an excellent hedge against inflation because it retains its value even when prices are rising. That's because gold is scarce and there's only so much of it in the world.

As demand for gold increases, so does its price. So if you're looking for an investment that'll hold its value over time, gold is a good choice.

Another benefit of gold investing is that it diversifies your portfolio. Because gold performs differently than stocks and other assets, owning gold can help reduce your overall risk.

For example, if stock prices are falling but gold prices are rising, your gold investments can offset some of your losses in other areas.

This diversification can help you weather market volatility and protect your wealth over time.

The Possible Consequences of a Wealth Transfer, and Why Gold May Be the Answer

Many economists, financial advisors and money managers agree an enormous wealth transfer is looming on the horizon. This transfer could be a gradual one, or it could come suddenly.

Regardless of the form this transfer takes, those who had the foresight to invest their wealth in gold, silver and other precious metals will reap the benefits. But what kind of consequences could this wealth transfer have? Let's take a look...

Deflation

Deflation occurs when prices drop due to a decrease in demand or an increase in supply. Deflation leads to decreased economic growth as well as higher unemployment rates.

Gold can help protect against deflation because its value remains constant over time. Since gold isn't affected by inflation or deflation, investors can rest assured their investments will remain safe no matter what happens with the economy.

Inflation

Inflation is when prices rise due to an increase in demand or a decrease in supply. Inflation has both positive and negative effects on the economy.

While it encourages spending since people believe prices will continue to rise, it also discourages saving since money loses its purchasing power over time.

Gold can help protect against inflation because its value increases when other currencies are devalued due to inflationary pressures. This makes gold an attractive asset for investors who want to hedge against inflationary risks.

Stagflation

Stagflation is a combination of high unemployment rates and high inflation rates that occur simultaneously within an economy. Stagflation often occurs during times of crisis such as wars or recessions, which lead to increased government spending and decreased consumer spending at the same time. Gold can help protect against stagflation since its value tends to remain relatively stable even during times of economic turmoil.

This makes gold a good choice for investors looking for stability in their portfolios during uncertain times.

Hyperinflation
Hyperinflation is extremely high levels of inflation that occur over short periods of time, often less than a year. Hyperinflation usually occurs when governments print too much money in an effort to stimulate the economy, without taking measures to control spending and debt levels simultaneously.

Since hyperinflations often lead to rapid devaluations of currencies, gold can provide investors with protection from these sudden drops in currency values by maintaining its value even during times of economic upheaval caused by hyperinflations.

Whatever form this potential wealth transfer takes (deflation, inflation, stagflation or hyperinflation), those who had the foresight to move their wealth into safe havens like gold are likely going to reap benefits from this inevitable event, whether it comes gradually or is suddenly triggered by another event.

Gold has always been seen as a store of value during times of economic uncertainty because it maintains its purchasing power no matter what type of economic environment, we find ourselves in—deflationary, inflationary or otherwise!

With all this said, now is an excellent time for investors looking for protection against uncertain economic times ahead to consider investing some part their wealth into physical precious metals like gold and silver.

How the Big Boys Always Win in Times of Financial Upheaval

We've all heard it before: the rich get richer, the poor get poorer. It's a phrase that's been around for centuries, but it's especially relevant today.

There's evidence to suggest whenever there's an enormous financial upheaval and wealth transfer, the wealthiest individuals always come out on top. To understand why this happens, let's take a look at how real interest rates affect society when they become negative.

What are Negative Real Interest Rates?

Negative real interest rates occur when short-term interest rates fall below inflation, meaning borrowers are actually being paid to borrow money.

This phenomenon incentivises people to take on more debt and risk because they're being rewarded for doing so. This creates a dangerous cycle of overborrowing and excessive risk-taking that can eventually lead to a financial crisis.

How Does This Affect Wealth Distribution?

In times of economic turmoil, those with more resources have access to better investments and opportunities, allowing them to leverage their wealth for even greater gain.

On the other hand, those with fewer resources are forced to make decisions with higher levels of risk due to their limited options, which often results in greater losses than gains.

As such, these unequal opportunities create a widening gap between wealthy investors and everyday people who just want to make sure their savings will last through retirement.

The Role of Central Banks

One major factor contributing to this inequality is central banks like the Federal Reserve and the European Central Bank.

These institutions have used negative real interest rates as a way to stimulate economic growth in times of crisis—but these policies don't always work as intended.

Instead, they often lead to further wealth inequality, as well as asset bubbles that eventually burst and cause chaos in global markets.

It's undeniable that when there's an enormous financial upheaval or great wealth transfer, the big boys always win—and if you look at all the golden parachutes awarded to executives who presided over our recent banking crisis, you can see how true this statement really is.

To stay ahead of the curve during times of economic turmoil, gold investors should be aware of how real interest rates affect society, especially when they turn negative, and be prepared for any sudden shifts in the market that could affect their assets or investments negatively.

By understanding how central banks shape our economy using negative real interest rates and other policy tools, we can gain insight into how wealth distribution works, and hopefully use this knowledge to protect our own finances in uncertain times.

Good Debt vs. Bad Debt: Why It's Important to Make the Right Choice

In today's world, it can be tempting to take advantage of a home equity loan or credit card offer in order to purchase items you may not necessarily need. However, there's a difference between good debt and bad debt.

Bad debt works against you and can ultimately lead to financial strain, while good debt works for you and can help you build wealth over time. Let's dive into what makes them different.

The Difference Between Good Debt and Bad Debt

Good debt is typically associated with borrowing money that'll increase your net worth in the long run, such as an investment loan or mortgage.

When used properly, these types of loans can help you grow your income by investing in assets like property or shares that'll appreciate over time.

On the other hand, bad debt is any loan taken out for something that quickly depreciates in value, such as a car or a TV. Instead of building wealth, bad debt turns into a liability costing more than it initially provided due to interest payments associated with the loan itself.

It's important to note that borrowing money isn't always a bad thing. In fact, there are certain circumstances when taking out a loan could actually be beneficial.

For example, if you invest in gold through a loan from your bank or broker and prices rise over time, as they historically tend to do, you could end up paying off your loan while making money at the same time!

This type of leveraging has been used by gold investors for years and can be incredibly lucrative when done right, so don't be afraid to borrow responsibly if it means growing your wealth down the line.

Ultimately, it's important to understand the difference between good debt and bad debt before signing any contracts or taking out any loans.

Good debt has the potential to increase your net worth over time, while bad debt can become an expensive burden on future finances.

Remember: use loans wisely, and always weigh both short-term pleasure with long-term financial security before making any decisions! A little bit of caution now could mean saving yourself from lots of stress later on down the road.

James's Chapter Summary for the Busy Bee (Or a Quick Recap)

The Sad Reality of Our Political System

🧈🚫: No real government freebies.

🏛️💰: Taxpayers fund politicians' promises.

⏰4: Leaders ignore long-term issues.

📉📜: Government aid can fail.

💪🚫: Advocate self-reliance.

The Problem with Promises

🆘🏛️: Public expects government solutions.

💼📉: Bailouts burden taxpayers.

The Government's Role

🛡️🚫💼: Government for defence, not bailouts.

💸🔄: Poor government spending hurts economy.

Big Government is Bad for Business

GB📊: Large UK government wastes resources.

💷🔥: Big government, big cost.

📚🚫: Red tape causes inefficiency.

🔑📉: Gold mitigates inflation.

The Benefits of Gold Investing

✨💰: Gold resists inflation.

📈📉: Gold stabilizes portfolios.

The Possible Consequences of a Wealth Transfer, and Why Gold May Be the Answer

💵📉: Gold's consistent value in deflation.

💵📈: Inflation boosts gold appeal.

💸🚀: In hyperinflation, gold stands firm.

How the Big Boys Always Win in Times of Financial Upheaval

🎩💰🔄: The wealthy thrive in chaos.

📉💶: Negative rates benefit rich.

The Role of Central Banks

🏢🌐: Negative rates can hurt economy and widen wealth gaps.

Good Debt vs. Bad Debt 💳🔄: Good debt builds wealth; bad debt drains it.

"Gold has always been the bedrock upon which the sands of fiat currencies shift and slide."

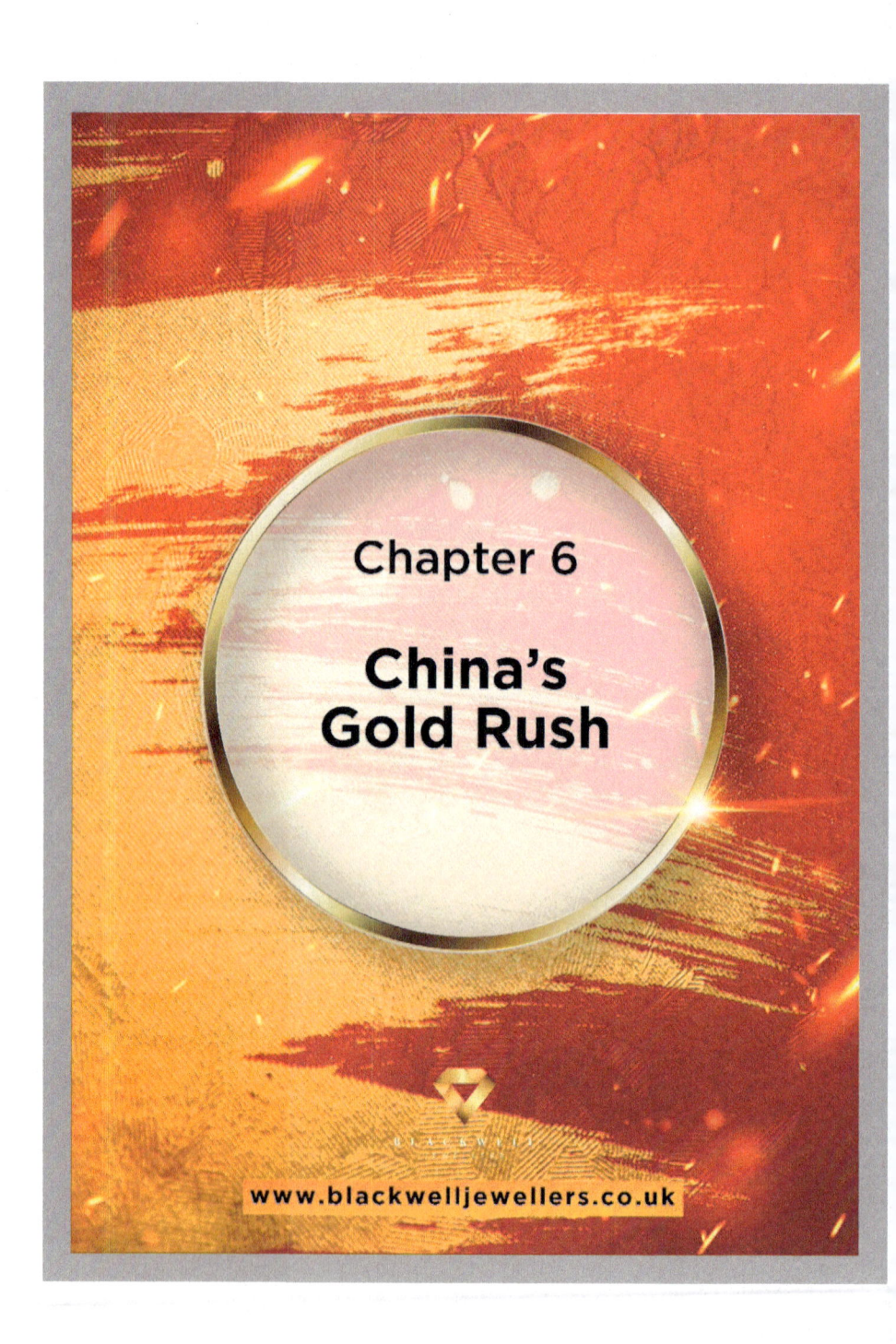

Chapter 6

China's Gold Rush

"James's Fun Facts"

"Ever wonder why astronauts have that golden visor?

Gold reflects harmful radiation. So, not only stylish, but also quite handy!"

Chapter 6

China's Gold Rush

Introduction

In the grand theatre of global economics, one might compare gold to a seasoned lead actor.

A character that, time and time again, never ceases to grab our attention with its flair and its dramatic performance amidst changing times.

In recent decades, however, the script took an intriguing turn, with a new character emerging from the ensemble cast – China.

Let's rewind a bit to better understand this shift. For years leading up to 2008, it was as if gold had become a forgotten relic in the world's central banks.

Picture huge vaults, stacked with bars of the yellow metal, sitting under dust covers, unloved and overlooked as institutions around the world sold off their reserves. Then, something unexpected happened.

Post-2008, the same banks performed a swift about-face. Gold was once again the belle of the ball, with central banks scrambling to accumulate it.

But that wasn't the surprising part. It was China, a newcomer, which emerged as a major player, dramatically changing the dynamics of the gold bull market.

This shift is an economic story worth its weight in gold, literally. It's a story of how, in a relatively short span of time, China transitioned from the sidelines of the gold market to centre stage.

An integral part of this story is the changes that have occurred in China over the last couple of decades, making it a protagonist in the global gold drama.

China's Transition to Gold

Change can be subtle, creeping in so gradually that it's hardly noticeable until it's irreversibly transformed the landscape.

Or it can be drastic, swift, and so profound that it leaves an indelible mark on history.

China's transition to gold was the latter, a breathtaking journey that saw the country become a global powerhouse in the gold market.

Until 1982, one might have been surprised to learn that it was illegal to sell gold jewellery in China, and gold bars were contraband until 2000.

Back then, the colour of wealth in China was red, symbolizing good luck and fortune.

But the turn of the millennium saw a shift in policy and sentiment, leading to a gold rush in the most populous nation on the planet.

In a few short years, China evolved from a country where gold ownership was heavily restricted, to becoming the world's largest producer and importer of gold.

That's right.

This sleeping dragon not only started mining and producing more gold than any other country but also began importing it at a scale that left other nations in the dust.

It was as if China had developed an insatiable appetite for the yellow metal, an appetite that showed no signs of abating.

This dramatic shift can be largely credited to the increase in wealth among Chinese households.

The economic reforms implemented in the late 20th century started bearing fruit, and China saw an explosion in wealth.

With growing affluence came a desire for solid investments, a need for a store of value, and nothing embodied that better than gold.

But it wasn't just about wealth accumulation; it was also about a newfound love for precious metals such as gold and silver.

This love was not just a flash in the pan; it was deep-rooted and strategic.

Chinese consumers, the government, and businesses alike recognized the value of tangible assets, particularly gold, as a hedge against economic uncertainty and volatility.

The economic landscape had changed, and gold was the ticket to wealth preservation and appreciation.

That's quite a transformative journey, right?

But there's more to this story of China's rise as a gold superpower and how it's reshaping the global gold market.

People's Bank of China's Golden Appetite

If you thought the gold fever among China's populace was fascinating, wait until you hear about what the People's Bank of China (PBOC) has been up to. Picture this: it's 2009, and the world is still reeling from the aftermath of the Global Financial Crisis.

Amidst this economic turmoil, the PBOC makes a move that sends ripples through the global gold market. They start buying gold, and not just a few bars here and there.

We're talking substantial quantities, enough to significantly bolster their reserves.

Yet, here's where it gets even more intriguing. Rumour has it that the PBOC's official gold hoarding might just be the tip of the iceberg.

You see, there's quite a bit of speculation that they've been accumulating gold reserves in secrecy, far beyond what they publicly report. It's like an economic thriller, isn't it?

A state-owned central bank playing cloak-and-dagger with the global market.

As for how much gold they've quietly stacked away, that's the million-dollar—or should I say million-ounce question. No one knows the exact amount, and the PBOC isn't exactly sharing its ledger with the world. But let's be clear here.

Whether it's smoke and mirrors or a solid strategy, there's no doubt that the PBOC's actions have serious implications for the global gold market.

Why all the hush-hush, you ask?

Well, many believe it's part of a grander vision. The PBOC aims to make the yuan a world reserve currency, a contender to the US dollar.

And to do that, they're betting on gold. It's a bold move, but then again, nothing about China's rise in the gold market has been less than audacious.

IV. The Boom of Gold Jewellery and Investments

With the PBOC taking the lead, it's no surprise that the Chinese public has also caught the gold bug. It's as if the entire nation has been gripped by gold fever, sparking a boom in both gold jewellery and investments tied to gold.

From Shanghai to Shenzhen, Beijing to Guangzhou, you'd be hard-pressed to find someone who doesn't have a portion of their wealth in gold.

Picture bustling jewellery stores, their displays glittering with intricate gold ornaments, from necklaces and bangles to earrings and rings.

Then there's the growing popularity of exchange-traded funds (ETFs) tied to bullion spot prices, as more Chinese investors turn to these investment vehicles to get exposure to gold without the need for physical storage.

What's driving this boom, you ask?

Well, Chinese investors aren't just enamoured by the shine and lustre of gold. They recognize its value as a safe-haven asset, especially when contrasted with riskier paper investments like stocks or bonds.

You see, gold has this fantastic quality where its value remains fairly stable, even when political turmoil, economic uncertainty, or even pandemics rattle global markets. It's like the rock of Gibraltar amidst a tumultuous sea.

The demand for gold in China, whether as jewellery or as an investment, is not a passing trend. Instead, it's a strategic move by a nation that has seen the ups and downs of economic volatility and is looking to safeguard its wealth.

It's a shift that underscores the growing importance of China, not just as an exporter or manufacturer, but as an influential player in global commodity markets.

As we peer into the crystal ball of future trends, one thing is clear. China's appetite for gold is set to keep growing.

Whether it's the PBOC's secretive gold acquisitions, or the Chinese public's increasing love for gold jewellery and investments, the world can expect China to remain a significant player in the gold market for the foreseeable future.

China's Golden Impact and Speculation

Now that we've covered the who and the how, it's time to delve into the question that's probably on your mind: "What does all this mean?"

When it comes to global gold markets, China is no longer just a spectator; it's in the game, and it's playing to win. From households hoarding gold bars to the PBOC's undisclosed accumulation, China's actions are more than just a domestic trend.

They're sending out ripples across the world, and it's time we paid attention.

Imagine this: the PBOC decides to open its vaults and reveal the true extent of its gold reserves. If the rumours are true, and they've been secretly stockpiling gold at a rate far exceeding what they've publicly reported, this could send a shockwave through the global economy.

On one hand, it might lead to a surge in gold prices, given the sudden realization that a significant amount of the world's gold is tied up in China's vaults.

On the other hand, it could raise questions about the reliability of other countries' reported gold reserves and potentially spark a new gold rush among central banks worldwide.

Talk about stirring the pot!

But that's not all. Remember how we mentioned that China's goal is to make the yuan a global reserve currency?

Well, if it can back its currency with significant gold reserves, it might just be able to give the US dollar a run for its money.

The mere speculation of this possibility could lead to shifts in the foreign exchange markets, impacting trade, investment, and economic stability across the globe.

As for the Chinese public, their love for gold is more than just a cultural fascination or a quest for personal wealth.

It's a reflection of their distrust in volatile paper investments, which can be as fickle as the weather, and their faith in tangible assets like gold, which has been a symbol of wealth and security for centuries.

But what does this mean for global markets? Well, as China's demand for gold continues to surge, we can expect an impact on gold prices worldwide.

The increasing demand could drive up prices, while the preference for physical gold could lead to a drain on global gold supplies.

This could potentially influence gold mining operations, investment strategies, and even geopolitical relations.

But it's not just about economics. China's gold rush is a testament to its people's resilience and adaptability. It's a narrative of how a country that once outlawed the ownership of gold has transformed into a significant global player in the gold market.

It's a story of determination, strategic planning, and the pursuit of financial security against the backdrop of a rapidly changing world.

Looking ahead, one can't help but wonder: What's next in China's golden saga?

Will the PBOC reveal its secret hoard?

Will the yuan become a global reserve currency?

How will the world react?

Will other countries follow suit and increase their gold reserves?

While we don't have all the answers, one thing is certain. The Chinese Dragon has woken up to the allure of gold, and it's not going to go back to sleep anytime soon.

As we watch this golden drama unfold, let's remember the words of the ancient Chinese philosopher Lao Tzu: "A journey of a thousand miles begins with a single step."

China took that step into the world of gold two decades ago, and it has been a riveting journey ever since.

With its increasing appetite for gold, strategic hoarding by its central bank, and a booming market for gold jewellery and investments, China's influence on the global gold market is set to grow.

Its actions and policies could shape the future of gold, and by extension, the global economy.

So, whether you're an investor, a policy-maker, a gold enthusiast, or someone who loves a good economic thriller, keep your eyes on China.

The country's gold rush might just be getting started, and trust me, it's a spectacle you don't want to miss.

That wraps up our deep dive into China's gold rush. We've explored the twists and turns of this golden tale, from the draconian laws of the past to the strategic manoeuvres of the present.

And as we stand on the precipice of an uncertain future, one thing's for sure: the story of China and gold is far from over.

It's a continuing saga of strategy, speculation, and, above all, resilience. And I can't wait to see what the next chapter holds.

James's Chapter Summary for the Busy Bee (Or a Quick Recap)

🌍🎭 - **Global Gold Stage:**

Experiencing the theatre of gold's global influence with China's rising dominance.

🏛️🟡 - **Banking Revival:**

Feeling the magnetic pull between central banks and gold, especially post-2008.

CN📈 - **Ascending Dragon:**

Watching China's meteoric rise from the gold market's periphery to its epicentre.

🚫📅 - **Historical Restraints:**

Reflecting on the time when China's gates were firmly shut against gold sales.

🐲💛 - **Golden Turnaround**:

Being a part of China's sudden embrace of gold, in production and imports alike.

🏛️🍽️ - **Insatiable Cravings**

: Sensing the PBOC's intensified chase for gold amid global uncertainties.

🔍😶 - Hidden Treasure?:

Venturing into whispers of China's concealed gold, which might overshadow official figures.

8. 📿✨ - Glistening Trends:

Marvelling at China's sweeping gold jewellery trend that adds sparkle to its streets.

✅🟡 - Golden Investments:

Noticing the gleam in Chinese eyes as gold ETFs carve their niche in investment portfolios.

10. CN🔒 - Defensive Strategy:

Feeling the heartbeat of China as it leans on gold, its bulwark against tumultuous waves of financial storms.

11. 🌍📈 - Market Resonance:

Tuning into the ripple effects as China strums its chords in the global gold market symphony.

"Central Banking is a Coordinated Currency Counterfeiting Cartel That Runs The world.."

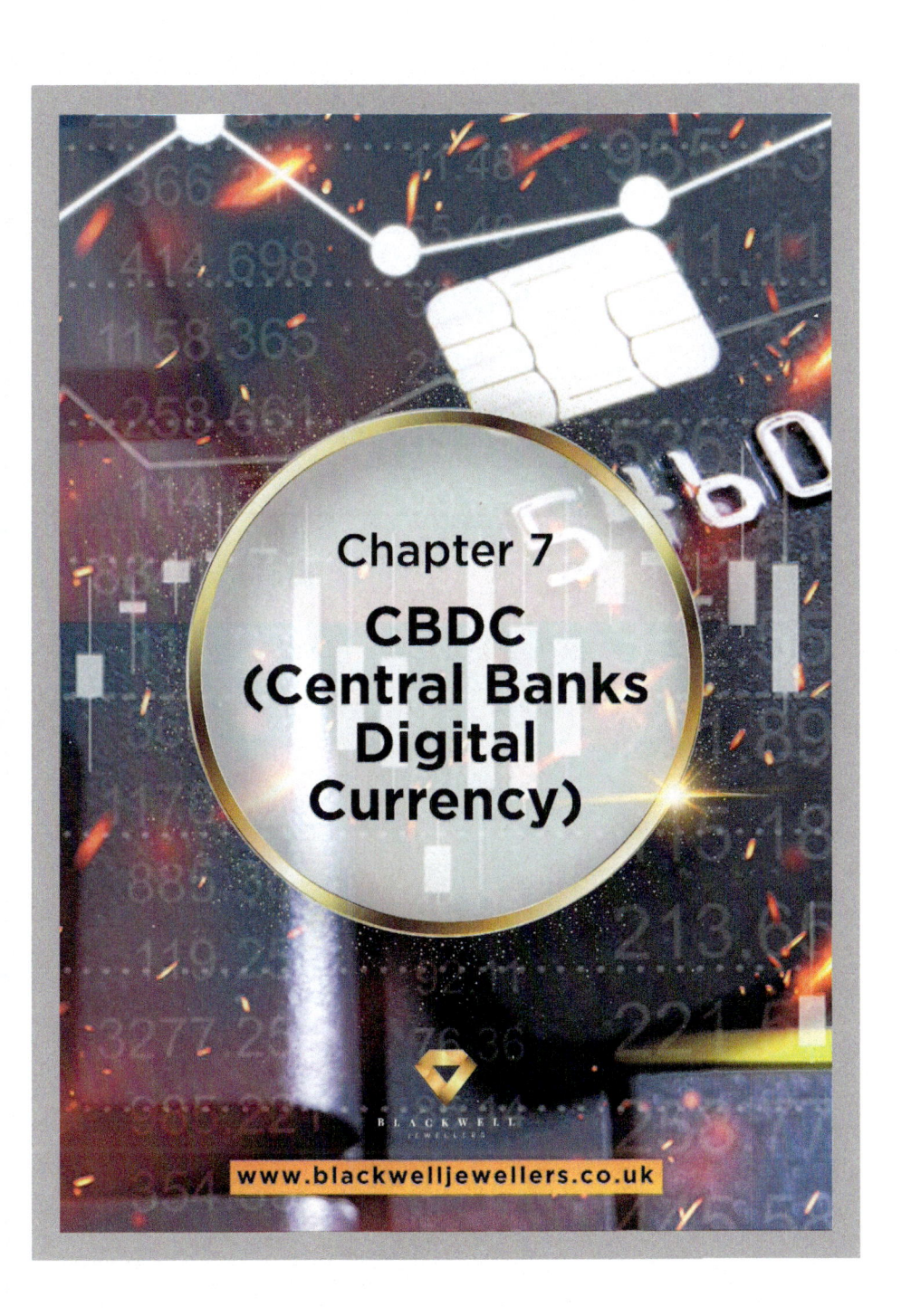

Chapter 7

CBDC (Central Banks Digital Currency)

"James's Fun Facts"

"When too much money is printed,

Not only do things get pricier, but services like haircuts or tutoring get devalued. Suddenly, your hours of hard work aren't worth as much.

The cheek!"

Chapter 7

CBDC (Central Banks Digital Currency)

I couldn't write a book about precious metals and banks without a brief chapter about CBDCs (central banks digital currency)—YET another way to control us.

The thought of this makes my blood boil, but I'll save that for another rant.

Ok, sit back as we embark on yet another exciting adventure in the world of finance.

This time, we're going digital, and more specifically, we're diving headfirst into the realm of CBDCs, or Central Bank Digital Currencies.

You see, CBDCs are all the rage right now, especially with the surge in digital payments and cryptocurrencies.

Oh, I hear you asking, "Wait, what exactly are CBDCs?"

Well, CBDCs are like your regular banknotes, only they're digital. They're the equivalent of money, minted in the world of ones and zeros.

These digital currencies are issued and regulated by central banks, like the Federal Reserve in the U.S., or the Bank of England in the UK.

Just picture it: a digital pound or a digital dollar, backed by the confidence we have in these established financial institutions.

CBDCs have been around for a little while, but it's only in the past few years that they've truly started to grab attention.

With digital transactions becoming the norm rather than the exception, CBDCs have found their moment to shine. And you know what else?

With the rise of cryptocurrencies, like Bitcoin and Ethereum, people are now more open to the idea of digital money.

But hey, why am I, a gold enthusiast, so interested in these digital currencies?

Well, it's pretty simple.

The arrival of CBDCs could have a direct impact on our beloved shiny metal. You see, if these digital currencies become popular, they could potentially influence the demand and value of gold.

Just think about it. Gold has traditionally been a safe haven, a store of value, especially in times of economic uncertainty.

Now, imagine if there was a digital alternative that offered similar benefits and was easy to use. It might make gold less appealing to some investors.

But don't get too alarmed. The views are quite mixed on this one. Some experts think that CBDCs could replace gold as a store of value, while others believe that gold and CBDCs could coexist peacefully, each with their own unique advantages.

The one thing that everyone agrees on, though, is that CBDCs are something to keep an eye on. Especially if you've got a stake in the gold market.

So, strap in, as we explore this exciting digital frontier. It's going to be one heck of a ride, and I promise to keep it as engaging and jargon-free as possible.

Now, are you ready to journey into the world of CBDCs?

Then let's get cracking!

Okay, let's delve deeper into this world of CBDCs. So, what are they really?

As I briefly mentioned earlier, Central Bank Digital Currencies, or CBDCs, are digital currencies issued and backed by central banks. They are not some weird invention from a sci-fi movie, but a real-world concept that could change our financial future.

CBDCs can come in different forms. They can either be digital versions of existing fiat currencies like dollars, euros, pounds, you name it.

Or they can be completely new digital currencies. Just imagine having a "FedCoin" or a "BritCoin". No, this isn't an episode of Black Mirror, it's a plausible future with CBDCs.

Now here's where it gets a bit techy. Some central banks are considering using blockchain technology, the same technology that underpins cryptocurrencies like Bitcoin, to issue their CBDCs.

Blockchain is essentially a decentralized ledger that records transactions across many computers. It's secure, transparent, and incredibly efficient, which makes it pretty appealing for something like a CBDC.

But why are we even considering digital currencies in the first place?

Well, one of the main reasons is to provide a digital alternative to cash. We live in a digital age, my friends. We shop online, work online, even socialize online.

So why not also have our money online?

And no, I'm not talking about online banking or digital payment platforms. I'm talking about digital currencies that could potentially replace physical cash for everyday transactions.

But it's not just about convenience. CBDCs could also be beneficial for individuals who do not have access to traditional banking services, often referred to as the 'unbanked'.

With a CBDC, these individuals could have a safe and regulated form of money that they can use for transactions, store for future use, or even save for that rainy day.

Imagine the potential of bringing banking services to every nook and cranny of the world. It could be revolutionary.

Moreover, CBDCs could make the financial system more efficient and secure by reducing the need for intermediaries like banks.

Transactions could be quicker, cheaper, and more secure. The same qualities that make blockchain attractive for CBDCs make them attractive for a more efficient financial system.

Of course. It's important to note that while I find the world of CBDCs fascinating and potentially transformative, I also harbour some reservations.

From my perspective, CBDCs represent yet another way for institutions to exert control over individuals.

In a world where CBDCs reign, every transaction we make could be monitored, traced, and, ultimately, controlled.

If our entire financial life becomes digitized, it leaves us vulnerable to surveillance and potentially even manipulation.

It's as if we are on a slippery slope towards a dystopian future where freedom, anonymity, and privacy in our economic lives could become relics of the past.

This viewpoint, however, is my personal one, and I do not wish to sway your judgement prematurely.

The future of CBDCs, much like any other financial innovation, is still being written and remains far from certain.

As such, I encourage you to absorb the information we're discussing, reflect upon it, and form your own perspective.

We'll be diving deeper into the world of CBDCs, and I hope these insights will help you make sense of the shifts happening within our financial systems.

While I have my concerns, it is undeniable that CBDCs could bring significant benefits to many, and it's that balance that we need to consider when forming an opinion on this matter.

Keep reading, keep questioning, and most importantly, keep an open mind as we continue this journey of exploration and understanding.

With all the facts and perspectives at hand, I trust you'll be able to make an informed decision about the potential future of CBDCs. Let's continue to peel back the layers of this intriguing subject.

Alright, let's delve deeper into the dynamic world of CBDCs and their distinction from cryptocurrencies.

At first glance, CBDCs might seem pretty similar to cryptocurrencies like Bitcoin or Ethereum. After all, they're both digital and leverage similar technology, right?

However, the similarities stop there. The primary difference lies in their foundation. Cryptocurrencies are decentralised, meaning no central authority governs or regulates them.

On the contrary, CBDCs are the direct responsibility of central banks and, in that regard, are akin to digital banknotes.

You might be thinking, "Hang on, if we already have cash and banknotes, why do we need a digital version?"

Good question. Let's dive into that.

One compelling reason is financial inclusion. There are still vast swaths of the global population without access to traditional banking services.

CBDCs, being digital, could broaden the reach of financial services, providing access to those who are currently unbanked. That's a big deal. By making it easier for these individuals to engage in financial transactions, we're opening doors for economic growth and poverty reduction.

CBDCs are also inherently efficient and secure when it comes to transactions. Think about it. With CBDCs, transactions are practically instantaneous and can be done from anywhere in the world, as long as you have internet access.

You won't have to worry about bank hours, weekend interruptions, or transfer limits. This efficiency can save time for individuals and costs for businesses.

But that's not all. From a security standpoint, CBDCs utilize blockchain technology, a form of decentralized digital ledger.

This technology ensures that every transaction is transparent and can't be tampered with once it's been recorded on the blockchain. This transparency reduces the risk of fraud and builds trust in the financial system.

When it comes to controlling inflation and stabilising the economy, CBDCs could provide central banks with unprecedented tools.

By having a direct relationship with every citizen via a digital currency, central banks could implement monetary policy more effectively.

For instance, during an economic downturn, central banks could theoretically 'airdrop' funds directly into citizens' digital wallets, boosting consumer spending and stimulating the economy.

Furthermore, CBDCs could also add resilience to the payment system in times of crisis. Suppose there's a natural disaster that takes out power and disrupts traditional banking services. In that case, those with access to the internet through mobile data or other means can still make transactions using CBDCs.

That's a level of robustness that's tough to beat.

All these potential advantages paint an optimistic picture, don't they?

But hold on, let's not get ahead of ourselves. It's crucial to remember that these are current assumptions and the actual implementation and impacts of CBDCs may deviate from these expectations.

The journey to CBDCs will require careful navigation, as governments and central banks weigh the pros and cons and find ways to mitigate potential risks.

In summary, while CBDCs share surface similarities with cryptocurrencies, they are vastly different creatures with unique implications.

They offer tantalising prospects for financial inclusion, efficiency, security, and control over economic parameters.

But, just like every coin has two sides, CBDCs have their set of drawbacks too, which we'll explore next.

For now, keep an open mind and remember that the assumptions around CBDCs are still being tested and may not always hold true.

Let's now delve into the lesser-discussed side of the CBDC coin - the potential drawbacks and ethical considerations. Remember, any discussion about a new technology, especially one that could potentially redefine our financial system, isn't complete without addressing the potential pitfalls and concerns.

As we've discussed, CBDCs bring a lot of promise for financial inclusion, efficiency, and economic control. But remember, these are, for the most part, educated assumptions.

The reality of CBDCs might turn out to be a little different than the theoretical assumptions. For one, while blockchain technology offers a secure and transparent transaction environment, it's worth noting that the security of this system is not entirely foolproof.

The system is as secure as the weakest link, and if that link is exploited, it could have a domino effect. Central banks will have to work very hard to ensure that the blockchain systems they deploy are safe from potential cyber-attacks.

An important aspect to remember is that the world of finance, central banks, and digital currencies is quite complicated. A lot of the current discussions about CBDCs are exploratory and largely based on assumptions.

There is still a lot of work to be done to understand the potential implications, the risks, and how to manage these risks.

Central banks and governments worldwide are researching and running pilot projects to learn more about CBDCs before making any significant commitments.

And now, let's get into the nitty-gritty of the potential drawbacks of CBDCs.

The first concern that comes to mind is the loss of transaction anonymity due to traceability. With physical cash, your transactions are largely untraceable, providing a level of privacy.

However, with CBDCs, every transaction you make will be recorded on a digital ledger. While this traceability can aid in fraud prevention, it also means that your every financial move can be tracked and traced back to you.

This raises serious questions about privacy, especially in countries with a history of government surveillance.

Next up is the imminent disappearance of physical cash and the issue of negative interest rates. Currently, if a bank imposes negative interest rates, you have the option to withdraw your cash and hold it physically to avoid being charged.

However, in a world where CBDCs have replaced physical cash, that option disappears. Your digital cash will be subject to whatever policies the central bank enforces, including potentially unfavourable interest rates.

Another aspect worth discussing is the programmability of CBDCs. With the move towards digital currency, central banks can make money 'programmable'.

In theory, they could set rules and parameters on how, when, and where the digital currency can be used. This control could potentially be used to direct economic activity or even as a tool for sanctions or control over economies.

Lastly, we must address the elephant in the room: the ethical issues around CBDCs. With the issues of traceability, programmability, and the absence of physical cash, we enter the realm of personalized monetary policy. Imagine a world where the government can control your spending by adjusting the interest rate on your digital cash.

This raises serious ethical questions about privacy, freedom, and control that societies will need to grapple with.

In conclusion, CBDCs offer a great deal of potential, but they also come with serious concerns. It's not just about technical feasibility or economic benefits.

It's also about societal impact, individual freedom, and privacy.

We're heading into uncharted waters, and it's essential to be aware of both the potential benefits and drawbacks.

Keep an eye on developments in this space. But for now, hold onto your physical wallets - they're not obsolete just yet.

James's Chapter Summary for the Busy Bee (Or a Quick Recap)

🌍 Introduction to CBDCs

Gateway to Digital Finance: Explore the emerging realm of Central Bank Digital Currencies, their origin, and their potential role in the global financial landscape.

📈 Economic Impacts of CBDCs

Shaping the Economy: Dive into the transformative economic implications of CBDCs, from boosting financial inclusion to providing central banks with novel monetary tools.

🌐 Global Digital Currency

Cross-border Transactions: Unpack how CBDCs can facilitate instantaneous global transactions, eliminating traditional banking delays and promoting international trade.

💻 Going Digital

Currency Evolution: Witness the shift from tangible cash to digital currencies, controlled and issued by central banks, and understand their foundational differences.

🤖 Blockchain Tech

Decentralized Assurance: Explore the intricate world of blockchain, the backbone of CBDCs, ensuring unparalleled transparency and security in transactions.

👁 Privacy vs. Transparency

Surveillance Concerns: Delve into the double-edged sword of digital ledger technology, balancing transaction traceability with concerns over personal financial privacy.

⚖️ The CBDC Balancing Act

Weighing Pros & Cons: Assess the challenges and benefits of CBDCs, emphasizing the decisions central banks must make concerning financial stability and inclusivity.

🚧 CBDC Implementation Challenges

A Road with Barriers: Understand the potential pitfalls, technical challenges, and the strategic steps towards the full adoption and acceptance of CBDCs.

😕 Ethical Dimensions of CBDCs

Beyond Practicality: Engage with the philosophical, ethical, and societal implications of CBDCs, from concerns over surveillance to the nature of financial freedom.

🔄 Future of Money

Horizons of Currency: Reflect on the broader impact of CBDCs on the future of money, commerce, and societies, and what it means for our physical wallets and the very notion of value.

*"When governments print money,
they forge chains of inflation;
when we invest in gold, we claim
the keys to financial freedom."*

Chapter 8
Property vs. Precious Metals

www.blackwelljewellers.co.uk

Chapter 8

Property vs. Precious Metals

Introduction: The Tangible Assets Tango

When it comes to the bustling dance floor of investments, there's something magnetic about the sway of tangible assets.

It's a dance many investors have been drawn to, from old school moguls to the fresh-faced mavericks making their first investment steps.

Why, you ask?

Well, there's a sense of security, a touch of the 'real', that these assets bring to the party.

Imagine the whirlwind of the economy: currencies in fluctuation, stocks taking a nosedive, and digital realms leaving many scratching their heads.

Amidst all this, the weight of a gold bar in your hand or the solid feel of a brick from your own property has a reassuring permanence.

It's like a trusty dance partner amidst the chaotic waltz of the economy. You know they've got your back, no matter how tricky the moves get.

And hey, in the realm of tangible assets, there are some pretty tantalizing options. I mean, sure, I might not own a patch of the moon (though how cool would that be?), but there's nothing quite like telling your mates, "Yep, I've got a stash of gold bars," or "I just invested in this property downtown." That's the allure, the undeniable tug of the tangible.

So, whether you're a seasoned investor or just tapping into the rhythm, read on, because this is one section you won't want to miss.

A Glimmering Overview: Gold and Silver in the Property Game

Gold and silver have an undeniable allure. Throughout history, they've been symbols of wealth and security.

In today's ever-evolving digital landscape, there's something reassuring about these tangible assets.

They remain steadfast, their value often unaffected by the unpredictable sways of economic shifts.

When discussing tangible investments, real estate inevitably enters the conversation. Owning a piece of land or property is a powerful asset; it offers potential rental income and appreciation over time.

But alongside property, gold and silver hold their own as reliable investments. Their tangible nature means they're not just numbers on a screen but real, hold-in-your-hand assets.

With the rise of Central Bank Digital Currencies (CBDCs) and the digital transformation of money, there's an increasing appreciation for the tangibility of gold and silver.

In a way, they serve as a counterbalance to the abstract nature of digital currencies.

However, it's essential to remember that while gold and silver are stable assets, they don't offer active returns like property can. Property can be a source of continual income if rented out, while gold and silver are more like safety nets, preserving wealth rather than actively growing it.

In summary, gold and silver bring stability and a touch of timelessness to an investment portfolio, while properties provide a potential for active growth.

Together, they offer a balanced approach to tangible investing, combining the old-world charm of precious metals with the dynamic potential of real estate.

Steady as a Rock: The Allure of Property

Ever heard the phrase, "They're not making any more land"? It's true. While the digital realm is expanding with things like cryptocurrencies and online businesses, the physical world's dimensions are pretty fixed.

This scarcity is what gives property its inherent value.

Real Estate: A House, a Holiday, and a Handsome Income

Step into the world of property, and you're stepping onto a stage of multiple opportunities. For starters, it can be a roof over your head—a place to call home.

And there's a unique sense of pride in knowing you own a piece of the Earth. Want to get away from it all?

If you have a holiday home, you don't need to scout for deals on hotel rooms—you have a personal retreat waiting.

But here's the kicker: real estate isn't just about living spaces. It can become a source of income.

With the right property in a suitable location, you can rent it out. This not only covers your mortgage payments (if you have them) but can also net you a tidy profit each month.

The Silent Growth: How Property Appreciates Over Time

While metals like gold and silver have their flashy moments in the market, real estate often appreciates quietly in the background.

Think of it like a plant. You might not notice its growth day by day, but give it a year or five, and it's flourished remarkably.

That's property for you. It's both a safety net—protecting your wealth against inflation—and a trampoline, offering potential leaps in value.

Certain factors can accelerate this growth. Urban development, infrastructure projects, and even the simple passage of time can make land and buildings more valuable.

Buy in an area today that becomes tomorrow's hotspot, and you've hit the jackpot.

The Revelation: The Endgame Isn't Just Shiny Metals

While precious metals offer a sense of security and are a brilliant strategy in the investment game, let's clear the air: the ultimate goal for many isn't just to hoard shiny coins.

It's to use the wealth accumulated from those metals to lay the foundation for a property empire.

Imagine turning a few gold bars today into multiple properties in the future!

It's like a game of Monopoly, but instead of paper money and game cards, you're dealing with actual gold and real houses.

To sum it up, while precious metals get the spotlight for their glitter and glamour, real estate silently builds empires. If played right, the two can dance together in a perfect symphony of strategic investment.

The Strategy: Leveraging Metals to Master Property

Investing might feel like a giant game of chess at times. Just like every piece has its role in the grand strategy of the game, every investment avenue has its unique strengths and advantages. Let's talk about how precious metals, the knights in our chess game, can gallop ahead and open up real opportunities in the property market, the ultimate king.

Historical Glimpses: Comparing Housing and Metal Markets

A trip down memory lane shows us an intriguing dance between the housing and precious metal markets.

There have been moments when housing prices surged, driven by factors like demand and low interest rates.

At the same time, the value of gold and silver has had its dazzling peaks, often riding waves of economic uncertainty or inflationary fears.

While both markets have their ups and downs, it's the relative movements between them that offer savvy investors opportunities.

For instance, there were times when the housing market plateaued or dipped, but metals shone brightly.

Vice versa, there have been instances where housing boomed while metals remained stable or even declined.

The Leverage Lesson: How Gold and Silver Can Be a Ticket to More Property

Now, here's where the magic happens. Suppose you've astutely invested in gold and silver during their ascent. When these metals appreciate significantly in value, they offer a powerful leverage point.

Instead of selling them off for quick cash, think bigger. How about converting that increased value into more significant property assets?

Remember, while gold and silver don't directly offer cash flows like rental income, they can be a vessel to amplify your investment reach.

The rise in their value can become your ticket to securing property at favourable prices, and in larger quantities than if you were to directly invest your initial capital in real estate.

A Hypothetical Hop: "Imagine Turning Your £100,000 into Five Houses, Not Just One. Here's How..."

Let's play with some numbers for clarity. Imagine you started with £100,000. Instead of directly buying a single property, you dived into the gold and silver markets.

Fast forward a few years, and with the right market conditions, let's say your investment has doubled or even tripled.

Now, armed with a significantly larger sum from your metal sales, you enter the property market.

That initial £100,000, thanks to your metals, now has the buying power that could get you multiple properties.

Instead of a lone house, you could be looking at a small collection of real estate assets, each with the potential for rental income and further appreciation.

And that's the beauty of a well-thought-out strategy. By leveraging the power of metals at the right time, you can catapult your way into the property market, expanding your empire in ways you might not have thought possible initially.

Risks, Rewards, and the Real Deal

Diving into the world of investments feels a bit like embarking on a grand adventure. There are exciting highs, daunting lows, and the thrill of the journey in between.

Like any expedition, it's essential to have a map—a clear understanding of the terrain you're navigating. Let's explore the landscape of investing in precious metals and property, marking out the pitfalls and pointing towards the peaks.

The Double-Edged Sword: The Volatility and Risks of Precious Metals

Investing in precious metals might seem like you're stashing away a timeless treasure, but remember, even gold and silver can tarnish momentarily in the face of market storms.

They're known for their volatility. Economic changes, global tensions, or even speculation can send prices on roller-coaster rides.

However, this volatility isn't necessarily a villain. For the nimble and informed investor, these price movements can present buying opportunities. The key? Stay informed, be patient, and have a clear strategy.

Playing the Long Game: Why Metals Can Be a Calculated Risk with Property as the Prize

So, why endure the turbulent waters of precious metals when there are calmer investment seas to sail?

The answer lies in the horizon. Metals, especially when viewed as a medium to a property-focused end, can be a game-changing strategy.

Think of it like this: the undulations in the metals market, when played right, could help you amass a wealth that's disproportionately larger than your initial investment.

This can position you to dive into the property world with a weightier wallet, allowing you to snap up properties that would've otherwise been out of reach.

But this approach is not about swift sprints—it's a marathon. It requires endurance, foresight, and a clear understanding of both the metals and property markets.

The trick is to buy metals when they're undervalued and then pivot to property at the opportune moment.

"It's Not Just About the Metal; It's About What the Metal Can Manifest."

In the end, the glitter of gold or the sheen of silver isn't the endgame.

They're tools, conduits towards a larger, more stable goal. And what's that?

The steady hum of passive income from real estate, the tangible assurance of bricks and mortar, and the pride of property ownership.

Remember, every investment carries risks. But with careful planning, a dash of patience, and an eye on the bigger picture, you can transform these risks into rewards.

After all, isn't the aim of this adventure to build a legacy?

And there's nothing quite as foundational, both literally and figuratively, as property.

So, let those metals pave your path to a prosperous property portfolio.

Because, ultimately, what's more golden than steady, passive income?

James's Chapter Summary for the Busy Bee (Or a Quick Recap)

🕴 Introduction: The Tangible Assets Tango

Investors are drawn to the security and tangibility of assets like gold and property amidst the volatile economic landscape.

✨ A Glimmering Overview: Gold and Silver in the Property Game

Despite the digital age's growth, gold and silver maintain their allure, complementing the dynamism of property investments.

🏠 Steady as a Rock: The Allure of Property

The finite nature of land and its inherent value stands in contrast to the ever-expanding digital realm.

🏠 Real Estate: A House, a Holiday, and a Handsome Income

Beyond shelter, properties can be income sources, offering rental profits and appreciating quietly over time.

🌱 The Silent Growth: How Property Appreciates Over Time

Real estate's value often grows subtly but surely, with various factors propelling its worth, making it a reliable investment.

💼 A Hypothetical Hop: "Imagine Turning Your £100,000 into Five Houses, Not Just One. Here's How..."

A strategic investment in metals, when timed correctly, can multiply one's buying power in the real estate market.

🏔️ Risks, Rewards, and the Real Deal

Investments are akin to adventures, with highs and lows. A clear strategy is essential when navigating between metals and real estate.

⚖️ The Double-Edged Sword: The Volatility and Risks of Precious Metals

Precious metals, though valuable, are volatile. However, savvy investors can leverage this volatility as an opportunity.

🏁 Playing the Long Game: Why Metals Can Be a Calculated Risk with Property as the Prize

Investing in metals with a long-term perspective can pave the way for sizable property acquisitions in the future.

⛏️ "It's Not Just About the Metal; It's About What the Metal Can Manifest."

Gold and silver are tools leading towards a grander goal: the stability and passive income from real estate investments.

"Gold doesn't yield to the whims of man-made systems. Its value is as timeless as the universe itself."

- Famous Philosopher

Chapter 9

The Intensity of the Wealth Transfer: It's No Joke!

"James's Fun Facts"

"Central banks and gold have a love-hate relationship.

While they hoard tonnes of it, they've sometimes sold huge quantities, causing market crashes. Mixed signals, much?"

Chapter 9

The Intensity of the Wealth Transfer: It's No Joke!

When one asset class is topping out and another is bottoming out, an intense wealth transfer takes place.

This transfer of wealth doesn't go unnoticed either.

It's like watching a herd of people chasing after yesterday's hot investment class even though the big gains have already been made.

To understand what this historical transfer of wealth looks like and how it affects gold investors, let's dive into the details.

Herd Mentality

It's human nature to want to be part of a winning team, and that's especially true when it comes to investing.

People often get caught up in the hype and excitement of a rising stock market or a booming housing market, and they don't want to miss out on the potential profits.

As a result, more and more people start pouring money into that particular asset class until it reaches its peak—at which point the entire cycle starts over again.

The Impact on Gold Investors

For gold investors, this kind of wealth transfer cycle can be both a blessing and a curse.

On one hand, gold investors benefit from the fact they can buy gold at low prices while everyone else is busy chasing after other assets, meaning they can make some big profits when the herd eventually dumps those other asset classes.

On the other hand, these investors must also contend with increased competition for gold when those same asset classes start tanking, which could drive up prices before they're able to purchase.

In short, understanding how wealth transfers work is an important part of being a successful gold investor.

By recognising when asset classes are reaching their peaks or bottoms, you can position yourself for maximum success in any given investment cycle. And potentially make huge profits along the way!

So if you're looking to invest in gold but don't know where to start, start by keeping your eyes open for signs of an impending wealth transfer so you can get in on the action before everyone else does!

Why Gold?

The appeal of investing in gold is simple: it's a tangible asset that's proven itself through millennia to be a reliable store of value.

In other words, its price isn't as volatile as many other investments.

It's held its value over long periods of time, and is seen as a safe haven for investors during times of economic uncertainty.

This makes it an attractive option for those looking to diversify their portfolios and protect themselves against potential losses due to market volatility or inflation.

Gold also appeals to investors because it's one of few investments that can be used as leverage when needed since it can easily be exchanged for cash at any time.

This means if you need access to liquidity, you can simply exchange your gold for cash, which can then be used for whatever purpose you may need.

Additionally, gold bullion coins are exempt from Capital Gains Taxes when sold, so this investment doesn't come with additional taxes like other investments do.

This makes gold an even more attractive option for many investors looking for ways to maximise their returns on investment.

How Do I Invest?

Investing in gold isn't complicated, but there are certain steps that should be taken before taking the plunge into this type of investment.

First and foremost, you should understand how prices fluctuate so you can make smart decisions when entering and exiting positions.

Researching historical trends will help give you an idea of what kind of returns you could expect from your investment over time.

Additionally, consulting with a professional will ensure your portfolio remains diversified across different types of assets.

This way, if one asset class takes a dive, your overall portfolio won't suffer too greatly from it.

Finally, don't forget to look into storage options. Investing in physical gold requires secure storage options, so make sure you research those thoroughly before making any commitments!

The great gold rush has been gaining momentum lately as savvy investors begin to realise just how profitable investing in gold can be, regardless of if they're looking for short-term gains or aiming towards long-term wealth-building goals.

With its ability to provide stability during times of economic turmoil, and its tax-exempt status when sold, now is definitely an opportune time to invest.

However, before doing so, make sure you conduct thorough research on both historical price trends, diversification, and storage options available, so your investments remain safe!

Echoes from the Past: The Footprints History Leaves Behind

It's an undeniable fact that the UK is experiencing a bit of a decline. Yes, I know, it's a hard pill to swallow, but hear me out.

The UK was once the ruler of the roost, the top dog, the big cheese in the empire game. In 1913, a staggering 412million people lived under the British Empire's rule, which accounted for a whopping 23% of the world's population at that time.

It still holds the record for the largest empire in human history, and at its zenith in 1920, it sprawled across an incredible 13.71million square miles—nearly a quarter of the world's land area!

Now let's hop across the pond and take a gander at our friends in America. Thanks to the US dollar's status as the world's reserve currency, Uncle Sam has a unique power: the ability to tax other nations through currency creation.

It's a nifty trick, but history, being the cheeky scamp that it is, tends to repeat itself. And just as with all empires before it, America has been slowly trading its freedoms for economic security.

It's becoming increasingly clear the US isn't so different from ancient Greece or Rome, or any other empire that fuelled its expansion with fiat currency.

Public works, social programmes, and wars funded by deficit spending is a potent cocktail that's spelled doom for empires throughout the ages.

Time and again, this lethal concoction has led to the downfall of even the mightiest of empires.

For these reasons, and many more, the dollar's days as the world's reserve currency are numbered, which means America's ability to dictate global economic policy through currency creation is also on borrowed time.

Things are looking bleak, and unfortunately, they're only going to get worse. Way back in 2006, the price of gold started to climb, and by 2008, it had skyrocketed to $869.75 an ounce during the financial crisis.

Then, just a few months later, it hit an all-time high of $1,000. If you think that was high, as I write this, gold is worth a whopping $2,033 per ounce.

That's not a good sign, not at all. With all the money being printed and pumped into the economy, gold is only going to keep getting more valuable.

Let me tell you something about this economic crisis: it's like when your mum tells you to put your toys away before your little brother breaks them. It's better to be early than too late, am I right?

That's why I've been moving my money around to prepare for what's coming. I used to invest in single stocks and try and make money that way—but failed miserably.

Instead, I'm all about those shiny precious metals like gold and silver. I've never got into Bitcoin, not because I'm a genius or anything, but because I like to hold things in my hand.

That being said, I am educating myself and I do think Bitcoin is something I will invest in.

And get this: gold is even more valuable now than it's ever been!

I've been lucky enough to have had my jewellery stores since 2006. I've been buying up gold ever since, and I'm still at it every month, not just for my stores but as an investment.

I'm pretty confident it's going to keep going up in value. If you want to be prepared like me, start investing in some gold and silver too!

I really do think the UK is teetering on the edge of a precipice. With economic turmoil and uncertainty on the horizon, fortunes will change hands at a remarkable rate.

Whether you're on the receiving end or not is entirely in your power. While the majority may face hardship, your circumstances could improve dramatically.

In this era of rapid transformation, the flow of information, ideas, emotions and knowledge is faster than ever, largely thanks to mass media and the internet. A rising tide of awareness is exposing the unethical nature of currency creation and the wealth shifts it triggers.

As more people race towards money, realising currency silently pilfers their wealth, those who have already secured their precious metals stand to gain significantly.

I'm not alone in considering the possibility the dollar, and consequently all fiat currencies, could falter. History shows fiat currencies have a survival rate of zero, and all currencies in the world today are fiat.

So, what would a wealth shift of this magnitude look like, and how would it affect you?

If global currencies were to collapse, the purchasing power of those without precious metals would transfer to those who do.

With major players currently amassing large amounts of precious metals, I fear a select few, already incredibly wealthy, could end up with all the spoils. Such a wealth transfer could lead to widespread subjugation.

However, during this tumultuous period, you have a unique chance to exponentially elevate your standard of living without taking on significant risk.

Most financial experts, even those within the precious metals community, argue precious metals aren't investments, but rather safe havens or wealth insurance.

Although it's true gold and silver always serve as a refuge against economic turbulence, there are fleeting moments in history when precious metals simultaneously act as a safe haven and the best-performing investment, delivering remarkable gains in purchasing power.

This impending wealth transfer is unprecedented, set against a backdrop of global imbalances that surpass anything we've ever witnessed.

Add to that the fact all the world's currencies are fiat and exhibiting signs of weakness, cracks in the global financial system.

I cannot stress enough the extraordinary nature of this moment in time. This is not simply a once-in-a-lifetime opportunity.

The upcoming wealth transfer will be unlike anything the world has ever experienced. I'm not taking a risk in saying that if you don't act after reading this book, you'll regret it for the rest of your days.

James's Chapter Summary for the Busy Bee (Or a Quick Recap)

📋 Asset Class Dynamics

The intense transfer of wealth observed when one asset class rises and another falls.

🏃 Herd Mentality in Investing

People often chase rising asset classes, even when the largest gains have been made.

💰 Gold Investors' Dilemma

Gold can be a boon during wealth transfers, but understanding its dynamics is crucial for success.

🔶 Why Gold?

Gold's enduring value, tax benefits, and liquidity make it an attractive investment.

📘 Investment Primer

Steps and considerations for venturing into gold investments.

🇬🇧 UK's Declining Dominance

A historical look at the UK's prominence and the implications of its current economic situation.

🇺🇸 US Economic Position

Concerns surrounding the US dollar's role as the world's reserve currency and its implications.

📉 Fiat Currency's Track Record

Historical evidence shows that all fiat currencies eventually fail, causing a major wealth shift.

⚖️ Potential Power Imbalance

A potential concentration of wealth could lead to a select few holding disproportionate power.

⏰ Urgency of the Moment

The upcoming wealth transfer's unique nature necessitates immediate action to seize the opportunity.

Chapter 10

Silver Fox

www.blackwelljewellers.co.uk

"James's Fun Facts"

" Gold melts at 1,064 degrees Celsius.

So, if you drop it into your tea, you should be alright.

Though, I wouldn't recommend it."

Chapter 10

Silver Fox

If gold is the age-old king of precious metals, silver is its dynamic, versatile cousin, aptly nicknamed the "Silver Fox" for its adaptability and charm.

Now, before we get all tangled in the silvery threads of its history, let's unravel the story of this fascinating metal that has, in so many ways, shaped our world.

Silver's Many Hats: From Cameras to Catalysts

At its core, silver is a multi-tasker. A metal that wears many hats—some shiny and reflective, others technical and industrial. It boasts being the most electrically and thermally conductive of all elements.

Plus, have you ever noticed how reflective silver is? This isn't just a vanity feature; it's a property harnessed in myriad modern technologies.

You might think of silver in jewellery or coins, but its role in photography might surprise you. Remember the pre-digital era?

When photographs had that special 'click' and 'flash'?

That was silver at play, creating magic on films and photographic paper.

The resume doesn't end there. Silver's in your batteries, possibly even in your medical devices, and certainly has its role in many of the electronics that make your life easier. Need clean water? Silver steps up in purification processes. And if you're keen on green energy, give silver a nod, for it plays a pivotal role in solar energy cells.

Market Dynamics: Silver's Supply Story

One might wonder: with such widespread use, what does that mean for silver's availability and price? Well, while gold loves to sit pretty in vaults and jewellery, silver's more of a workhorse.

It's heavily consumed in industrial processes, and this voracious appetite means we have to keep mining, refining, and producing it. That makes silver's supply narrative a bit tighter than golds.

When there's a surge in demand, silver's price tends to inch upwards. A dance of supply and demand, if you will, with silver often taking the lead.

Silver Through the Sands of Time: Its Golden Relationship

Silver's saga isn't just about today—it's about yesteryears too. Its track record as currency spans millennia. Yet, what's particularly intriguing is its age-old relationship with gold. You see, these two haven't always been on equal footing.

Historically, a ratio determined their relative value. Imagine 1 ounce of gold getting you 12 ounces of silver.

That wasn't plucked from thin air—it was the market's balancing act, gauging their worth based on their scarcity.

While gold might've been the reserved, elusive one (thanks to its rarity), silver was the people's metal. Its abundance made it the go-to for everyday transactions, while gold strutted its stuff for the big deals.

Now, these ratios haven't remained static. Market forces, like a gentle breeze or sometimes a gusty wind, have pushed the silver-gold ratio around. From 8:1 at times, stretching up to 16:1 at others, it's a dynamic figure, offering insights into both the metals and, more broadly, the economy.

The market will continue to discover new prices for gold and silver in the future. Understanding the ratio is an important tool in understanding the history of silver and the economy as a whole.

Silver Bull

The current silver market is ripe for a bull run. This time around, there are several factors that make this bull market different from any we've seen in the past.

One of the most significant differences is the sheer amount of money that's been printed in recent years. Central banks around the world have been pumping money into the economy, and this has led to inflationary pressures. As investors search for ways to protect their wealth from inflation, they're increasingly turning to precious metals, like silver.

Another factor that makes this bull market different from the past is that investors have learned from their mistakes. In the 1980s, many investors chased after gold and silver, buying them at high prices, only to sell them at a loss as the stock market took off in the 1990s.

But this time around, investors aren't making the same mistake. They're not selling silver to chase after stocks. Instead, they're buying silver as a hedge against inflation and a possible stock market crash.

Governments also play an important role in the current market as well. Throughout history, governments have been a major source of silver supply. They used to hold large stockpiles of silver and used it as coinage.

However, in recent years, governments have been selling off their silver holdings, artificially depressing the price. This trend has led to a situation where today governments around the world are effectively out of silver.

When you put all these factors together, it becomes clear the current silver market is on the cusp of a bull run. The combination of increasing demand and decreasing supply is a recipe for higher prices, and I believe this bull market will be the biggest yet.

The market is volatile, and there's risk involved, however, investing in silver at these low prices is an excellent opportunity to take advantage of a market on the verge of a major shift.

Many people might wonder why silver is so cheap right now when it should be worth so much more. The answer is that people have been conditioned to think silver should be cheap, and it's mainly because governments have been dumping their silver into the market for half a century.

This extra supply has had the effect of suppressing silver's price, and the low price has resulted in our consuming more silver than we produced for over half a century.

As of 2007, governments have pretty much run out of silver, and they've stopped selling just as investor interest is rising. But, as you may already know, there's almost no silver left for investors to buy. And again, Economics 101: when there's great demand and minimal supply, prices will skyrocket.

However, some might ask, "Won't they just mine more silver?" The short answer is yes, but most silver supplies don't come from silver-mining operations.

Rather, silver supplies are often a by-product of mining copper, lead, zinc and gold. In fact, about 75% of the supply of newly mined silver originates as a by-product of mining other metals.

This silver is a bonus to these mining companies, and as David Morgan points out, "A copper miner certainly is not going to throw the silver out." So they sell it on the market, but their business isn't dependent on the price of silver.

The burden to satisfy silver demand falls on the shoulders of what are known as primary silver producers—and they're a rare breed. Currently, silver mine production stands at a little over 500million ounces per year.

Primary silver producers only produce 25% of that, or 125million ounces per year. If you could freeze demand where it is today, and the primary silver producers were able to double production, it would take more than 15 years to get silver inventories back to the level they were in 1990.

Furthermore, it's not just about running out of above-ground silver, but also running out of silver in the ground too. Minable deposits of silver are becoming harder to find.

Ray De Motte, former President of Sterling Mining, recently said the ratio of minable silver to gold might be less than 8:1 today, versus 12:1, or greater, in the past. According to the US Geological Survey, at current rates of production, the two metals we'll run out of first are gold and silver. At these rates, gold reserves will be exhausted in 30 years, and silver in just 25.

When you invest in silver, it's important to be prepared for a lot of changes. I've been buying and investing since 2003, and I've had good times and bad.

Even though it's been volatile, I've held on and continued to add to my portfolio of silver and gold. The main reason I do this is because I need to have gold and silver as stock for my business as a jeweller.

Some people might wonder why I keep investing in silver, even when it's not a stable investment. The reason is that I've not met anyone who became rich by trading stocks all the time.

People new to investing often make the mistake of trying to get involved with the next big trend. But then they end up losing money because they buy when the stock is already high, then sell when it goes down low, incurring big losses.

There are many reasons why silver is a good investment opportunity. As silver is a scarce resource, which we're running out of it, and which is becoming harder to find and extract, the price of silver may very well be worth much more in the near future.

The price of silver is below the point where most primary producers can turn a profit, which means there's potential for the price to go up.

Keep in mind that silver hasn't reached its 1980s peak yet. This makes silver a good opportunity to purchase because it could have potential gain in purchasing power with the expansion of the money supply, and with inflation.

As I pen these very words, I find myself increasingly drawn to silver, though this, of course, is a matter of personal preference.

A word to the wise, if I may be so bold: when it comes to silver, always opt for the 0.999 fine variety. This is what we in the trade refer to as 'investment grade' silver—the very stuff that industry craves. And with global supplies dwindling, it's the silver they'll be willing to pay through the nose for.

A word of caution, however: steer clear of old US 90% silver coins—unless numismatics is your passion, in which case, by all means—and other forms of impure silver, such as sterling silver. You see, when you sell silver that's not 0.999 fine to a dealer, it's often destined for a refinery.

Between 1979 and 1981, when silver prices were soaring to unimaginable heights, so many people were selling silverware, jewellery and the like, along with 90% silver coins, that the silver refiners were utterly swamped for over a year.

Now I may not have a crystal ball, but I reckon history is bound to repeat itself. And when it does, your less-than-pure silver may very well sell at a significant discount compared to its more refined cousin.

James's Chapter Summary for the Busy Bee (Or a Quick Recap)

🦊 Introduction to the Silver Fox

Silver's adaptability and charm have earned it the nickname, playing various roles throughout history.

🎩 Silver's Multifaceted Roles

A versatile metal used in jewellery, photography, batteries, medical devices, electronics, water purification, and solar energy.

⚖️ Market Dynamics and Availability

While gold often remains stored, silver is heavily used industrially, impacting its availability and price.

⏳ Historical Context

Silver's storied past, including its relationship with gold, illustrates its prominence and the fluctuations in its value.

🔄 Silver-Gold Ratio

This dynamic relationship between gold and silver offers insights into broader economic conditions and the metals' respective values.

📈 The Coming Silver Bull Market

Several factors hint at an impending surge in silver prices, including money printing, inflation, previous investor behaviour's, and government interventions.

🏛 Government's Role in Silver's Value

Historically, government activities have impacted silver prices, especially with them selling off their reserves.

🌍 Global Silver Supply

A look at silver sources, the difference between primary silver producers and by-product production, and the challenge of meeting rising demands.

🌍 Declining Global Reserves

Silver and gold reserves are depleting fast. At current production rates, gold reserves will end in 30 years, silver even sooner at 25 years.

📊 Investment Insights and Silver's Worth

Investing in silver requires patience, especially amidst its volatility. Its scarcity and potential price growth make it appealing. Opt for the 0.999 fine 'investment grade' silver for higher returns. However, caution against old US 90% silver coins and impure forms is advised due to potential refining requirements and subsequent loss in value.

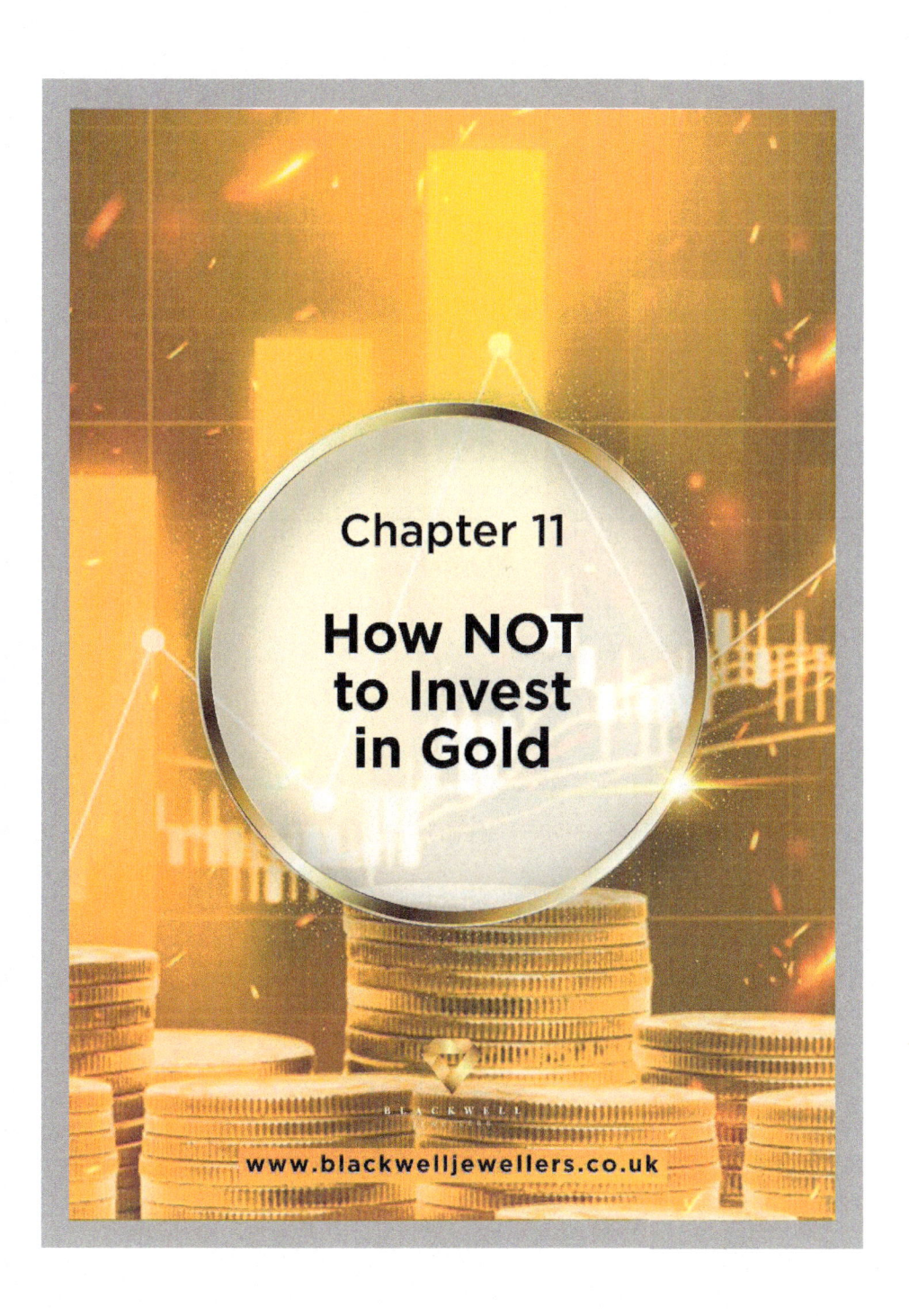

Chapter 11

How NOT to Invest in Gold

"James's Fun Facts"

"In the late 1800s, a chap named Sir Isaac Newton.

Who was the Warden of the Mint, set the gold price in England at £4.25 per ounce.

It stayed there for 200 years! Talk about setting a long-term trend."

Chapter 11

How NOT to Invest in Gold

I know, I know, you're probably thinking, "Oh, this all sounds easy and straightforward," but let me tell you, it can be a minefield out there. But don't worry, I'm here to guide you through the process of gold investing, and to help you avoid the pitfalls and traps many investors fall into.

Now before we dive into the nitty-gritty of how to make the most of your gold investments, let's take a moment to talk about the dangers and risks that come with investing in this precious metal. It's not the most exciting topic, but trust me, it's better to know what *not* to do.

First and foremost, there's always the risk of fraud.

Unfortunately, there are plenty of shady characters out there more than willing to take advantage of unsuspecting investors. Whether it's selling you 'gold' that's not actually gold, or charging exorbitant fees and commissions, these scammers will stop at nothing to separate you from your hard-earned cash.

When it comes to investing in precious metals, there's always the risk of running into a few bad apples. But fear not! By knowing what to look out for, you can safeguard yourself from falling victim to their tricks.

That's why in this chapter we'll not only be discussing the best ways to invest in gold, but also the potential dangers you should be aware of. Because as they say, an ounce of prevention is worth a pound of cure.

Pool Account or Certificate Programme

So, you've been doing your research and you've come across something called a 'pool account' or 'certificate programme'. You're thinking to yourself, "Wow, this sounds like a great idea!

I can invest in precious metals without having to worry about storage or security!"

Well, my friend, let me tell you, it's not all sunshine and rainbows when it comes to these types of investments. There are quite a few negatives you should be aware of before diving in headfirst.

First and foremost, there's the issue of ownership. When you invest in a pool account or certificate programme, you don't actually own the physical gold or silver. Instead, you're buying into a pool of precious metals managed by a third party.

This means you have no control over the storage or security of your investment, and you're completely at the mercy of the company or organisation running the programme.

Another downside is the lack of liquidity. Because you don't actually own the physical gold or silver, it can be difficult to access your investment or sell it when you want to. This means you could be stuck in the investment for a longer period of time than you'd planned.

And finally, there's the issue of fees and charges. Many pool accounts and certificate programmes come with high management fees, storage fees and other charges that can eat away at your investment. So it's important to be aware of these costs before you invest.

ETFs (Exchange-Traded Funds)

Exchange-traded funds, commonly known as ETFs, have become a popular choice among investors looking to gain exposure to various markets and asset classes, including precious metals.

However, before considering ETFs as a vehicle for investing in these precious metals, it's essential to understand the limitations and potential pitfalls of using them.

First and foremost, it's essential to understand that ETFs aren't actual physical holdings of the metal, but rather represent a claim on a specific amount of the metal held by the fund.

This means if the ETF isn't fully backed by the physical metal, it can lead to a situation where the value of the ETF may not match the price of the underlying metal.

Additionally, ETFs can be subject to tracking errors, where the price of the ETF doesn't perfectly match the price of the underlying asset.

This can be caused by a variety of factors, including the way the ETF is structured and the fees associated with the fund.

Another limitation of ETFs is that they're not as liquid as physical gold or silver, and they can also be subject to counterparty risk, which means the ETF provider or issuer could default or become insolvent.

In contrast, physical gold and silver are a tangible asset that can be held and stored, giving the investor full control over the asset, eliminating counterparty risk.

Moreover, owning physical gold and silver allows the investor to take advantage of the potential long-term appreciation, as well as the potential use as a hedge against economic or political uncertainty. In contrast, ETFs are subject to market fluctuations, and the investor isn't guaranteed any long-term appreciation.

While ETFs can provide a convenient and cost-effective way to gain exposure to the gold and silver markets, it's crucial to understand their limitations and potential pitfalls.

Ultimately, owning physical gold and silver may be a more secure and reliable option for those looking to invest in these precious metals. It's essential to do your research and fully understand the risks and benefits before making any investment decisions.

Numismatics: The Art of Collecting Coins

Numismatics, the art of collecting coins, medals and paper money, can be a fascinating hobby and investment opportunity, but it's important to approach with caution.

Numismatic coins are collector items, valued for their rarity, age, condition and historical significance.

While it may sound exciting to invest in a coin considered rare, it's important to keep in mind that not all numismatic coins will perform well as an investment.

In fact, many numismatic coins are overpriced and end up being worth less than what the collector paid for them.

Let me tell you about a customer of mine, let's call him Joe. Joe had always been fascinated by numismatics and decided to invest a considerable amount of money on some rare coins. But, even when the price of gold doubled, he still couldn't get his money back. He ended up stuck with a bunch of 'beautiful' coins worth less than what he'd paid for them. He learned the hard way that just because a coin is rare, doesn't necessarily mean it's a sound investment.

The numismatic market is full of potential pitfalls, from exaggerated claims of rarity and historical significance, to overpriced and over-graded coins. It's essential to do your research and understand the coin's rarity, historical significance and condition. It's also crucial to be aware of the market trends and potential risks involved.

Another thing to keep in mind is that the numismatic market can be highly speculative and subject to manipulation, where a coin's value is artificially inflated by dealers or investors looking to make a quick profit.

For the most rare and expensive coins, there will always be a strong demand from wealthy collectors, making them a solid investment.

However, for the majority of collector coins, the numismatic premium is highly dependent on the state of the economy and public sentiment.

It's important to note that dealer profits on numismatic coins can range from a modest 15% to a staggering 100%, or even more in the case of scams.

In contrast, bullion coins, valued solely on the spot price of the metal they're made from, typically have no numismatic premium and command a dealer profit of only 1% to 5%.

Have you ever heard of a coin becoming ultra-valuable just by someone giving it a bit of a once-over? Well, believe it or not, it's true! Coin grading services have the power to take a coin from drab to fab, from common to rare, and from worth a few pennies to worth a small fortune.

Take, for example, the American Gold and Silver Eagles. These coins may be minted by the millions, but thanks to the magical process of coin grading, they can become highly sought-after and valuable.

After being purchased at the US Mint, they're sent off to undergo rigorous inspection and grading.

And voila! Just like that, their value shoots right up, from selling for mere dollars, to fetching hundreds or even thousands. All thanks solely to their newfound 'uncirculated' status.

So next time you're looking to invest in a coin, remember coin grading services have the power to turn a common coin into a rare gem. It's like the fairy godmother of the coin world, turning pumpkins into golden carriages.

While a numismatic coin's value is derived from the desire and passion of a particular buyer, and prices can vary wildly, the value of a bullion coin is based on the metal's spot price, and the potential number of buyers can number in the millions, with prices more consistent.

In short, numismatic coins can be a potentially lucrative, but also a risky investment. As a result, it's important to be aware of the potential for scams and frauds in the numismatic market, so do your research before making a purchase.

As I research more about numismatics, I become increasingly convinced, with the exception of the oldest and rarest coins, that the entire numismatic business is little more than a con job. Therefore, I urge you to do your own research and make an informed decision before jumping in. It's always wise to diversify your portfolio and not put all your eggs in one basket, or you might end up with a basket full of 'beautiful' coins worth less than the price of the basket.

Commemorative Coins

If you've been watching TV or reading magazines lately, you may have come across an advert or two offering commemorative coins.

They look great and sound like a good investment—but buyer beware! Chances are these coins are nothing more than a scam. Let me try and explain why anniversary coins should always be treated with suspicion.

So what makes these commemorative coins so fishy? Well, it all comes down to the underlying economics.

Any company that can afford to pay for expensive advertising campaigns must be making huge profits, which means they're likely ripping off the people who buy their coins.

And if they don't even bother to make sure their products have any resale value, well... that's a pretty big red flag right there.

The fact is that most commemorative coins have absolutely no value beyond what people are willing to pay for them.

They're not backed by gold, silver nor any other precious metal, they don't appreciate in value over time, and they can't be exchanged for anything else of value.

In other words, you might as well just set your money on fire— you won't get much out of buying one of these 'commemorative coins' anyway.

The only thing these companies really care about is getting your money in exchange for their worthless product. That's why it's important to do your research before making any kind of investment decision, especially when it comes to gold investing.

If something looks too good to be true, chances are it probably is!

Sleazy Salespeople

Have you been hounded by phone scammers promising you the world but delivering nothing but heartache?

First of all, be wary of smooth-talking salespeople trying to lure you in with their so-called 'gold opportunities'. Remember: if it sounds too good to be true, it probably is.

And never, I repeat, *never* give out your phone number just to 'learn more' about an investment. A legitimate opportunity will be explained in full, in writing.

Another scam to watch out for is when someone pressures you into giving out your contact information with the promise of a 'free consultation' or 'call-back'.

My advice? Run in the opposite direction! Chances are they're just trying to get their hands on your personal details to scam you.

And last but not least, always remember to do your due diligence before investing in any type of asset, especially gold. Check out reviews from other investors, and make sure the company you're looking at has a good reputation and track record before committing any of your hard-earned cash. Trust me, it's better to be safe than sorry.

Scams

As a jeweller for over three decades, I've seen more scams than you can shake your diamond-studded stick at! From crooks trying to pass off 9ct coins as 22ct, to filling up hollow earrings with lead—there's no shortage of ingenuity when it comes to criminal activity.

But don't worry if all this deception has left you feeling unsure about the next piece of jewellery or your gold investment.

Luckily, my many experiences have helped me cultivate some sage advice on how to spot fraudulent practices in order make sure your money is safe.

Are you ready to outsmart those sneaky con artists and their devious scams? As gold investors, it's essential you're always on the lookout. After all, knowledge is power, and we're not going to let a few scammers make off with our hard-earned bullion!

Making Off with Your Bullion? Not So Fast!

One scam con artists struggle with is bullion coins. It's near impossible to replicate a full sovereign coin in another material and make it weigh 7.98g. So what do they do?

They usually go for the next best thing and counterfeit numismatic coins instead. As mentioned, numismatic coins are collectible coins with a greater value than their metal content because they're rare or have an interesting history behind them.

But be careful, just because something has been graded by an expert, doesn't mean it's real.

To ensure you're not being scammed, always double check the weight and dimensions of your gold bullion coins against reputable sources online or in print guides. A few hundredths of a gram can make all the difference between a real coin and a fake coin!

And remember: if it seems too good to be true, it probably is.

Certified Coins Beware!

Another trick con men like to use is making fake certified coins. Recently, I heard about people buying certified and slabbed coins online, only to find out later that the coins were fake.

How does this happen? The scammer will take high-quality, collectible coins, send them into a grading service, and get them back in tamper-proof slabs—but he doesn't keep them there for long!

The scammer takes out the real coin from its supposedly secure slab, then replaces it with a fake version, before sending it off to unsuspecting buyers.

If you want to avoid this scam, check if your seller has certification from third-party grading companies such as NGC (Numismatic Guaranty Corporation) or PCGS (Professional Coin Grading Service).

Also, be sure to ask for digital images of both sides of the coin before making any purchases—this way, you can double check things like design details and wear patterns yourself before handing over your cash.

Always trust your gut; if something seems fishy, it probably is.

Gold Bars (Sealed)

Another type of scam con men might use is sealed fake bars. They come in different sizes, but the problem is that you might buy a fake one if you can't take it out and feel or weigh it.

The best thing to do is avoid buying anything sealed unless you know who the person is or that it's a reliable source. If you need help, we have gold bars that are checked and hallmarked. You can contact me at jamesmarsh@blackwelljewellers.co.uk or on 0208 3015484.

Take your hands off MY gold.

It's a topic that's been discussed and debated for decades: could the government reclaim all the gold again, just like they did in 1933?

Well, as they say, the government can do what it wants. And unfortunately, if they decide to take all the gold, there's not much you nor I can do about it. But before you start stockpiling canned goods and building a bunker, let's take a closer look at the likelihood of such a scenario.

First of all, it's important to note that the government's decision to outlaw private gold ownership in 1933 was a response to the economic crisis of the Great Depression.

The idea was to stabilise the economy by increasing the money supply, which could only be done by increasing the amount of gold held by the government.

However, today's economy is vastly different from in 1933. Gold is no longer the backbone of the monetary system, and the government's ability to control the economy through monetary policy has improved significantly. Additionally, the global economy is now much more interconnected, and any move by the government to nationalise gold would likely have severe consequences on the international stage.

Another important factor to consider is that private gold ownership is now a well-established practice, and there are millions of people and institutions that own gold.

Outlawing private gold ownership would mean the government would have to seize the assets of millions of individuals and organisations. This would not only be incredibly difficult, but also incredibly unpopular.

It's also worth noting that gold is a widely used store of value, and it's held by investors, central banks and other institutions around the world. A move to nationalise gold would likely result in a significant drop in its value, which would have far-reaching consequences for the global economy.

In short, while it's possible the government could nationalise gold and outlaw its use and private ownership again, today's economic and political realities make such a move highly unlikely.

So while it's important to always be aware of potential risks, it's also important to keep things in perspective.

The government can do what it wants, but it's highly unlikely they'll be reclaiming all the gold again anytime soon.

But it's always good to be prepared and informed, so keep an eye on the news, and stay up to date with the latest developments in the world of gold and finance. In the meantime, it's safe to keep buying and stacking shiny coins and bars, and enjoy the benefits of being a gold owner!

James's Chapter Summary for the Busy Bee (Or a Quick Recap)

⚠️ Beware of the Risks

Investing in gold is filled with pitfalls and traps. Key risks include fraud and other deceptive practices from disreputable sellers and dealers.

🌊 Pool Account Pitfalls

Pool accounts and certificate programmes might seem convenient but pose ownership issues, lack of liquidity, and high fees, diminishing the value of your investment.

📊 ETF Limitations

While ETFs offer exposure to precious metals, they aren't tangible assets. They're susceptible to tracking errors, counterparty risks, and might not fully represent the underlying metal value.

💰 The Art (and Risk) of Numismatics

While numismatic coins can be beautiful and historic, they're often overpriced, speculative, and may not guarantee a sound return on investment.

🔍 Grading and Its Influence

Coin grading can elevate a coin's perceived value significantly, but investors should be wary of relying solely on grades for investment purposes.

🪙 Commemorative Coins:

Often showcased with impressive advertising, these coins might not provide a good return on investment and have little resale value.

💁‍♂️ Sleazy Salespeople:

Beware of smooth talkers offering too-good-to-be-true investment opportunities and always ask for detailed documentation.

🎭 Scams:

With a long career in jewellery, the author has seen various scams, from misrepresenting coin quality to selling deceptive jewellery items. Always stay vigilant.

⚖️ Certified Coins:

Even coins that are certified can be tampered with. Scammers might replace genuine coins in protective cases with fakes. Always verify before purchasing.

🏛️ Government and Gold:

Reflecting on the 1933 decision by the government to reclaim gold, the article reassures that today's economic conditions make such an event highly unlikely.

"The true power of gold lies not just in its shimmer but in its steadfast value amidst economic storms."

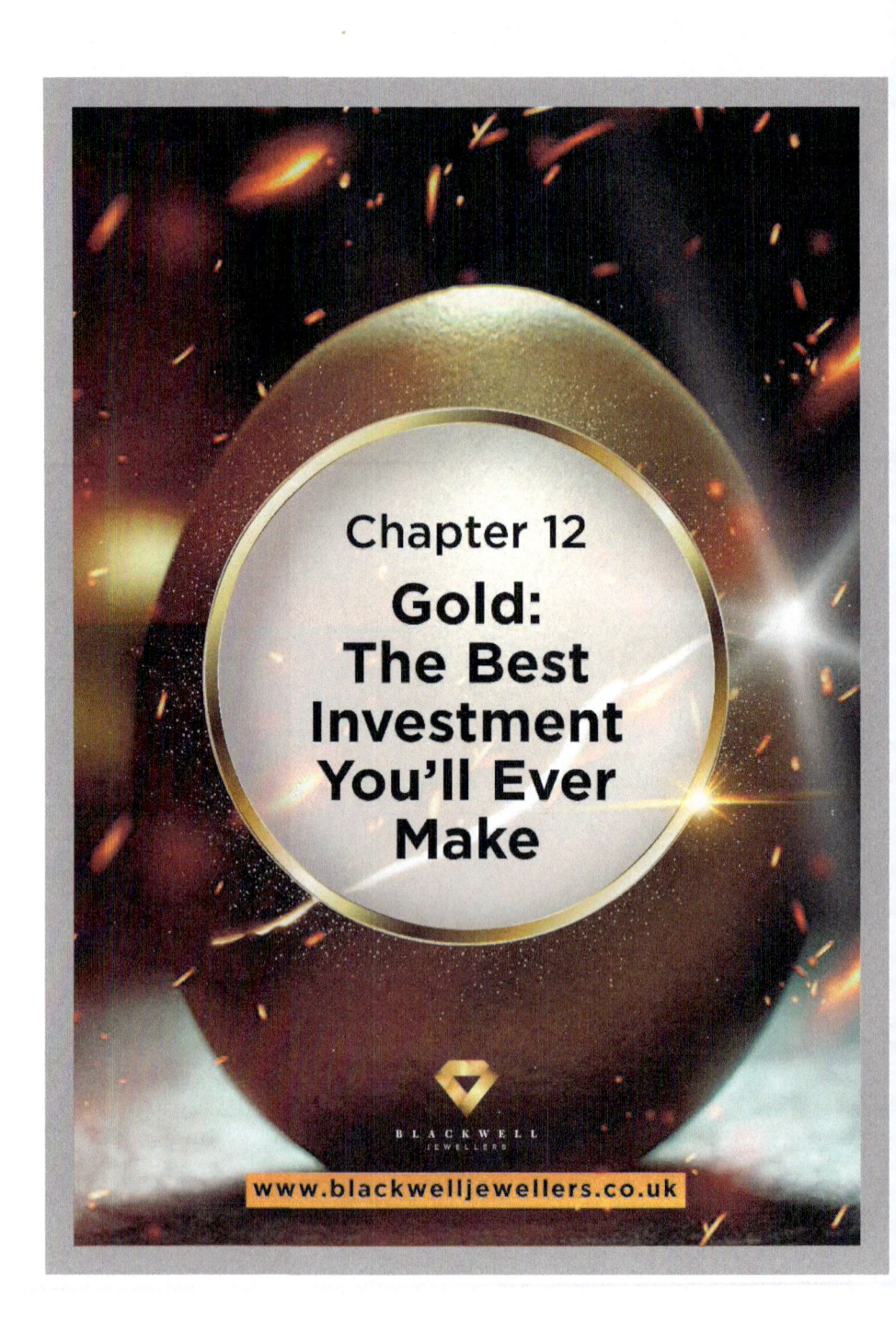

Chapter 12

Gold: The Best Investment You'll Ever Make

www.blackwelljewellers.co.uk

"James's Fun Facts"

"Now, if you think printing money is a modern thing, think again.

The Ancient Romans were doing it, diluting their gold and silver coins.

The result?

Rampant inflation. Classic move!"

Chapter 12

Gold: The Best Investment You'll Ever Make

I'm genuinely perplexed by how popular it is to knock gold these days. It's troubling that folks are being fed dodgy investment advice, and heart-breaking to witness people work their socks off their entire lives only to end up with meagre pension pots, their futures filled with disappointment and anxiety as hard-earned savings slowly rot in bank accounts offering insultingly low interest rates.

And yet, even with all these risks, I still see a whole generation discouraged from investing in gold. Why's that, then? The only reason I can think of is that gold is seen as a bit 'old-fashioned'.

It's laughable, really. Stone farmhouses are quite old-fashioned too, and they've been standing for centuries, while flimsy modern homes get blown down in a couple of decades.

Let's delve into the reasons why owning physical gold and silver is far superior to its digital form. By the time you've finished this quick round-up, you'll have a crystal-clear understanding of why gold remains the best investment you can make.

You might already be aware of these, and this might just be a little nudge to jog your memory. If so, I'm chuffed I've been able to give you a reminder.

A little heads-up: I don't claim to be a financial advisor; truth be told, I don't think many are worth their fees. I'm not one of those self-appointed 'investment gurus' either. I'm a practical, hands-on sort of bloke. While people are out there blabbering about the pros and cons of investing in this and that, I'm actually doing it and securing my family's future. And I'm doing it with gold.

You always own it. With physical gold and silver, you own the asset outright from day one, unlike property, which you'll never really own—see what happens when you stop paying council tax. There are no mortgages, leases or rent payments involved because you have 100% ownership.

It's easy to buy. Physical gold and silver are more straightforward to buy, and they come without risk of being frozen out due to technical issues, like with cryptocurrency, where transactions can take hours or days to complete due to high demand that puts strain on the system, causing delays in processing times.

It's easy to sell. When investment whizzes talk about 'liquid stocks' and high 'liquidity', they mean an investment that can be sold and offloaded quickly. Gold and silver are highly liquid assets. You can sell in a jiffy by popping down to the local jeweller or pawnbroker. Your investments can work for you as long as you want, or be sold quickly when needed.

It's easy to appraise. When dealing with diamonds, for example, a potential buyer needs an expert appraiser in order to determine its worth. Whereas with physical gold and silver, all you need is a simple scale in order to weigh it accurately and agree a price based on that weight.

Both buyers and sellers know exactly what they're dealing with right away, without needing additional expertise beyond basic maths skills to calculate prices per gram/oz based on current spot prices.

It's easy to liquidate. Physical gold and silver can easily be liquidated into cash since spot prices for precious metals fluctuate daily, allowing investors who wish to sell off their holdings to quickly turn them into cash.

It's easy to store. Physically storing gold and silver is much easier than storing a digital investment because it doesn't require any special technology or software like cryptocurrency does. All you need is a safe place where no one else can access it.

It has portability and transferability. Unlike other investments such as stocks, bonds, etc., investing in physical precious metals offers great portability and transferability, meaning they can be easily transported anywhere without any limitations imposed by governments, laws, etc.

It's low maintenance. Property investments? Don't get me started. Sure, you can charge tenants for some costs, but you can't escape nasty surprises—broken boilers, leaking taps, damaged plaster, worn carpets, etc. Canny investors know gold and silver maintenance costs are minimal, like having a friend who never lets you down.

It's a tangible asset. One of the key advantages of owning physical gold or silver is that it has real-world value that can't be reduced by market forces like stocks or bonds can be. This means even if the stock market crashes, your gold will still maintain its value due to its intrinsic worth as a tangible asset that can't be duplicated or devalued by outside forces beyond your control.

It can't be frozen. It's a sad fact of life that world governments can't always be trusted. In times of financial turmoil, they might overstep their boundaries. We've learned from history that governments can 'freeze' assets, bank accounts, and even deny wages. Pension schemes in particular are perpetually at risk. Gold is your insurance against all this malarkey. The government can't freeze your physical gold any more than they can any cash stashed under your mattress.

It can't be hacked. We've all heard horror stories of digital theft and identity fraud. Sly con men snatching property deeds, hackers on the other side of the globe draining bank accounts, and let's not get started on cryptocurrency investments. No one can swindle you out of your gold the way they can with property or digital assets.

It has no counterparty risk. With digital forms of currency such as Bitcoin, there could be counterparty risk involved, meaning someone could default on their payment, leaving you out of pocket. However, when dealing with physical precious metals, there's no counterparty involved, so this risk factor doesn't even exist.

It has no exchange rate risk. Since both buyers and sellers agree upon a price based on current spot prices, there's no exchange rate risk involved as everyone knows ahead of time exactly how much they'll pay/receive during each transaction.

It has no currency devaluation risk. Investing in tangible assets such as these provides protection against currency devaluation, which can occur during times when governments decide they need extra funds, resulting in them printing more money and reducing its overall value. Investing in physical precious metals can act as an inflation hedge too, helping protect against rising prices due to currency devaluation over time.

It has no third-party interference. With physical gold or silver, there are no third parties involved, making it easier for both parties without any interference. Banks, in their position as go-betweens, could interfere with transactions between buyers and sellers, as everything takes place directly between these institutions.

It has no tax implications. Depending on where you live, taxes may need to be paid when investing in certain assets. However, investing in physical precious metals doesn't necessarily incur any tax liabilities since many countries don't consider them taxable assets.

It has diversification benefits. Investing in physical precious metals can help diversify your portfolio. Different types of assets tend to behave differently during economic downturns, so having tangible investments such as these could help protect against losses should conditions worsen.

It's risk-free. This is the pièce de résistance, the big secret only few seem to grasp. Gold has been around for thousands of years, and its value has never plummeted to zero.

Banks crumble, property markets crash, people lose their savings overnight, companies go bankrupt—and let's not even mention the potential demise of cash as governments plot to replace it with their own digital currencies.

Through all these trials and tribulations, gold remains steadfast, a beacon of stability in a turbulent world. Gold was here before money and will be here long after.

There's only a limited amount of gold on our little blue planet; central banks can't just print more when they fancy! Gold is the investment that simply refuses to become worthless. Smart investors know that when it comes to putting their money somewhere safe, gold is the go-to.

Now I must confess my portfolio is rather heavily weighted towards physical precious metals, accounting for a substantial 50% to 60% of my investments.

Real estate comes in second, making up approximately 30%, with energy stocks and other commodities sharing a modest 5% to 10%. As for the remaining, that's tucked away in cold, hard cash. This approach has served me rather well.

Allow me to share with you one of my greatest joys in the realm of investments: the acquisition of physical gold and silver for safekeeping at home, segregated in a depository, or perhaps even offshore in an allocated account. Now why, you might ask, does this tickle my fancy so?

Well, it's quite simple, really. By choosing this path, you effectively sidestep the corporate financial industry's elaborate game of smoke and mirrors. Instead, you, my gold-loving friend, retain control of your hard-earned wealth and keep your investments shrouded in a veil of privacy, far from the meddling gaze of inquisitive onlookers.

And do you know what the most satisfying part of this whole endeavour is? The undeniable reality of the tangible treasure you possess. You can touch it, feel the weight of history in your hands, and revel in the knowledge you hold in your grasp not just any old asset, but real money—the sort that's withstood the test of time, maintaining its allure throughout the ages.

So, when you venture forth into the dazzling world of precious metals, remember you're not merely dabbling in investments; you're taking part in an age-old dance with wealth itself, one that grants you the luxury of privacy and the satisfaction of holding genuine value within your hands.

So, there you have it: why gold is the best investment you'll ever make. It's time to embrace this golden opportunity and secure your financial future. And when you do, you'll be grinning all the way to the bank (or your home safe).

James's Chapter Summary for the Busy Bee (Or a Quick Recap)

😐 Scepticism of Modern Views:

Many are dismissive of gold as an investment, often viewing it as outdated despite the unstable nature of contemporary financial instruments.

📜 Historic Resilience

: Much like ancient stone farmhouses that withstand time, gold has been a lasting and dependable asset throughout history.

👐 Tangibility:

Physical gold provides a sense of realness. Unlike digital assets, you can touch, feel, and appreciate its intrinsic value.

🏅 Owning Physical Gold:

You own physical gold outright from day one, without external financial entanglements like mortgages or taxes.

📉 Stability Against Market Forces:

Unlike stocks or digital currencies, gold's value doesn't plummet to zero, ensuring a reliable safety net.

🔒 Security and Privacy:

Gold provides an investment shielded from government interference, hacking risks, and the prying eyes of institutions.

🌍 Universal Value:

Gold's value isn't bound by country or currency, ensuring its worth remains recognized globally.

🚫 Less Interference:

There's no third-party involvement with gold, ensuring transactions aren't meddled with by banks or other institutions.

⏳ Test of Time:

Gold has withstood various economic crises, maintaining its value and allure throughout history.

🏆 Golden Opportunity:

Embracing gold as an investment is more than just a financial decision; it's an engagement with lasting wealth and value.

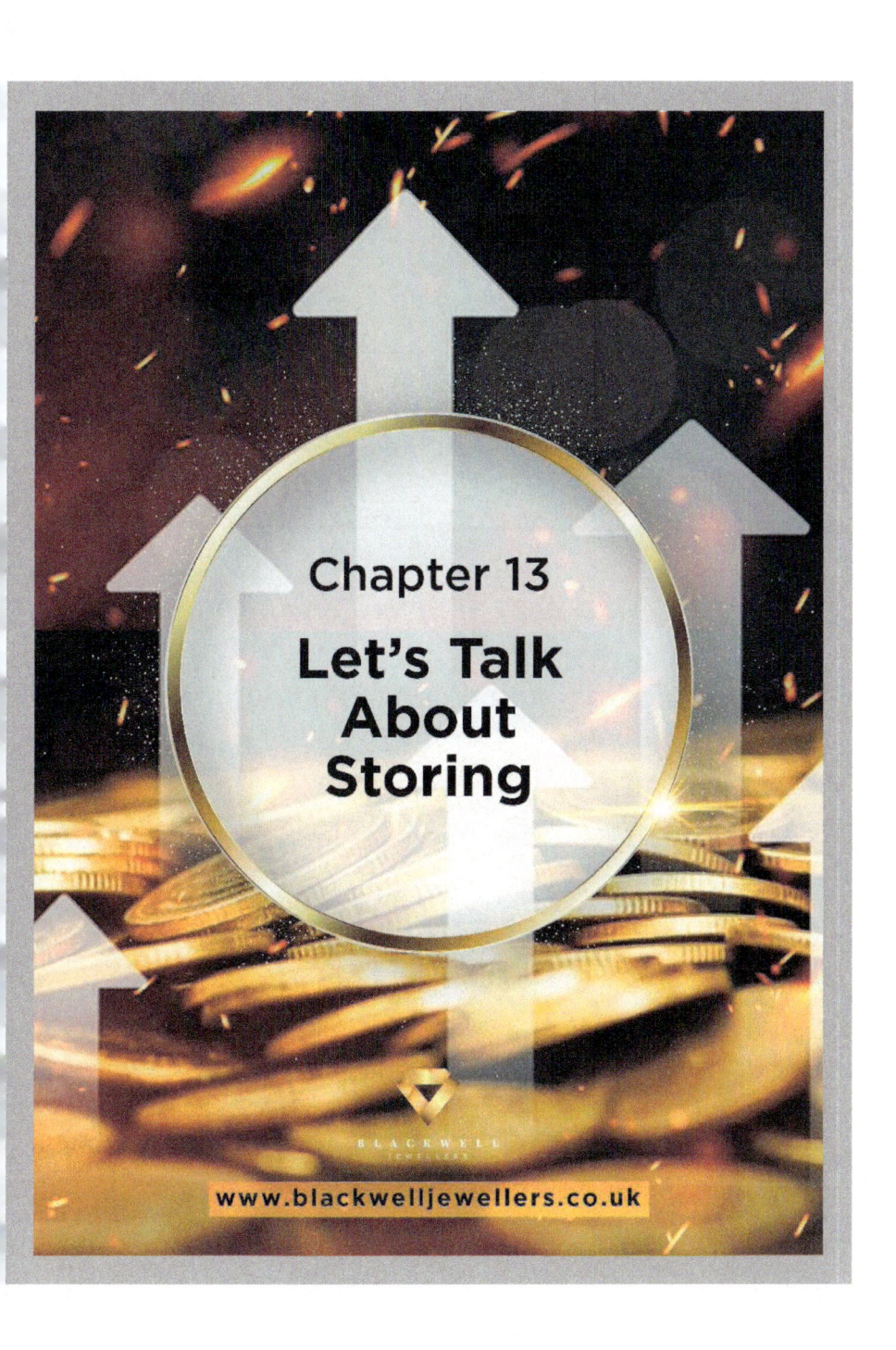

Chapter 13
Let's Talk About Storing

www.blackwelljewellers.co.uk

"James's Fun Facts"

The largest ever gold bar weighs 250 kg.

That's like holding 40 bowling balls made of pure gold! No need for the gym when you're lifting that."

Chapter 13

Let's Talk About Storing

One of the most pivotal moments you'll experience in your gold investment journey is when you physically hold your gold in your hands for the first time.

The weight, the sheen, the undeniable sense of value - it's all part of the allure of gold. But the realization quickly follows: where do you store such a precious commodity?

The storage aspect of investing in gold is an important one to consider. It's something that can make potential investors pause. After all, not everyone is equipped to store bars of gold at home like a modern-day pirate.

And yes, you're not wrong; if you decide to store your gold in a bank vault, there will be costs involved. However, before you get disheartened, let's put things into perspective.

The fear of storage costs is something that plagues many potential gold investors. It's the spectre at the feast that can sometimes make people think twice.

But here's the reality check: when you invest in stocks, do you not pay a variety of fees?

Think about fund managers, stockbrokers, financial advisors, trading platforms, and more.

So why does the idea of paying to keep your gold safe seem so alien and daunting? In reality, it's not that different from the fees associated with other investment assets. And the truth of the matter is, the costs associated with gold storage are quite minimal.

Why? Because the volume of gold you'll be storing is small. It's not like you're Fort Knox and need to worry about finding a space for countless bars of gold.

Consider this: a kilo of gold is worth around £50,000. That's a small volume, but an enormous amount of wealth. If you've amassed enough gold to start worrying about storage space, you're doing pretty well, mate!

And if you'd rather not pay someone else to keep your gold safe, there's always the option to store your gold at home.

Storing your gold at home can be as simple as investing in a robust, secure safe. There are countless options available, ranging from high-tech digital safes to classic dial combination safes. It's all about finding something that fits your needs and gives you peace of mind.

Now, you may be thinking: "Sure, James, I can buy a safe. But what if someone breaks in and steals it?" Fair point.

But remember, a good safe isn't just about keeping your gold out of sight. It's about making it so difficult to access that any potential thief would be deterred.

There's also the option of a safety deposit box at your local bank. It's a choice many people don't immediately consider when thinking about storing their gold, but it's a solid one.

A safety deposit box offers you an unparalleled level of security, and they're insured against theft or fire. Plus, they offer an impressive level of anonymity. No one knows what you have stored in there but you, and that's a comfort in itself. The best part?

Safety deposit boxes are not as expensive as you might think. For a nominal annual fee, you can ensure your gold is safely tucked away in a place equipped to handle its security. Banks like Metro Bank are known for their top-notch safety deposit box services.

But let's step back and think outside the box, so to speak. If the idea of storing your gold at a bank or in a home safe doesn't appeal to you, there are other options to consider. One such option is a hidden floor or wall safe.

These aren't your average safes. A hidden safe is designed to be installed in your home, completely hidden from view. It's as James Bond as it gets when it comes to gold storage. The idea is simple: you install the safe in a place where it's unlikely to be found, and it remains your secret.

However, if you decide to go down this route, make sure you discuss it with your insurance agent first. You'll want to ensure that your home insurance policy covers the contents of the safe in the unfortunate event of a theft or fire.

If you're going to store significant amounts of gold or silver at home, a safe - hidden or otherwise - is an investment worth making.

Professional safe companies can help you make the right choice.

They'll understand your needs and concerns and guide you through the process of choosing the best safe. With their advice, you can rest assured knowing your precious metals are in good hands.

It's worth noting that the storage decision you make may also depend on the amount of gold you own.

If you're a smaller investor, a home safe might be the best and most cost-effective solution. However, if you're dealing with larger quantities, the more robust safety measures offered by banks or professional storage facilities might be the better way to go.

Remember, every investor's needs are unique. But with a bit of research and careful planning, you can find the perfect storage solution for your gold.

For those of you who don't feel entirely comfortable storing large amounts of gold or silver at home or simply don't want to worry about it, there are specialized vault storage accounts that cater specifically to precious metals.

These accounts offer a variety of security levels and storage options to cater to different needs, sizes of investment, and comfort levels. Let's delve a little deeper into what these accounts entail.

Segregated vault storage is a storage account option that allows each customer's metals to be separated or 'segregated' from other customers' metals. This means that your gold is stored in its own allocated area within the vault, separate from all other investors' gold.

It's like having your own exclusive corner in the vault. This service provides an extra level of assurance as you'll know exactly where your gold is and that it's not mixed up with anyone else's assets.

Allocated vault storage, on the other hand, is a storage option where you own specific bars within a larger pool of metal held by the vault provider.

Unlike segregated storage, your gold might not have its own designated section in the vault. However, the exact bars that you own are documented and accounted for.

With this type of storage, you have the comfort of knowing that your gold is there, waiting for you when you need it, even if it's not in its own exclusive section of the vault.

Choosing between segregated and allocated vault storage can depend on a variety of factors. You might choose segregated storage if you want the psychological comfort of knowing your gold is separate from everyone else's.

On the other hand, allocated storage can sometimes be a more cost-effective option. Remember, the right choice is the one that fits your needs and gives you the most peace of mind.

Now, at this point, you may be wondering how you'd access your gold if it's stored in one of these vaults. Well, that's the beauty of these services.

They're designed to make it easy for you to access your gold whenever you need it. Whether you want to sell some of your gold or just want to check on it, you'll find that these services offer an efficient process to ensure you can do so with ease.

When it comes to safety and security, these vault storage facilities are second to none. We're talking about state-of-the-art security systems, round-the-clock surveillance, reinforced structures - the works.

These facilities take the safety of your investment as seriously as you do. After all, their reputation depends on it.

If you opt for a professional vault storage service, rest assured that the company's primary focus is on safeguarding your wealth.

This means your precious metals are not just stored; they are protected in a facility that is designed to withstand a variety of threats. Whether it's a potential theft, fire, or even natural disasters, these facilities are equipped to handle it all.

However, it's always essential to do your due diligence when choosing a vault storage provider.

Look for a company with a strong track record, positive customer reviews, and a commitment to transparency.

Ask questions about their storage process, access policies, insurance coverages, and costs involved. It's your wealth on the line, so don't hesitate to ask these questions.

No matter where or how you decide to store your gold, it's crucial to remember why you invested in the first place.

Gold offers you a tangible, stable, and valuable asset that can act as an insurance policy against economic uncertainty.

So, whether you choose a home safe, a safety deposit box, or a specialized vault storage account, remember the end goal: protecting your wealth.

In conclusion, storing your gold is just as important as purchasing it. You've invested in a commodity that has held its value throughout history, and it's crucial to ensure that it's safe.

It's not a decision to be taken lightly, but with careful consideration, you can find the best storage solution that offers security and peace of mind.

James's Chapter Summary for the Busy Bee (Or a Quick Recap)

🪙✨ - **First Touch:** Physically holding your gold for the first time, appreciating its weight and value.

🏠💭 - **Storage Dilemma:** The decision-making process of where to store gold, be it at home or elsewhere.

🏦💰 - **Banking Costs:** Delving into the costs associated with storing gold in a bank vault and comparing them with other investment fees.

🗄️💀 - **Safety Deposit Option:** The merits of using a safety deposit box at banks for its high level of security and discretion.

🏠🔒 - **Home Safes:** The variety and advantages of having a home safe, from digital to classic dial safes.

⚫🖼️ - **Hidden Treasures:** Exploring the intrigue and security of hidden floor or wall safes in homes.

🏦🔒 - **Vaulting Choices:** The specialized vault storage accounts and their two main types: segregated or allocated storage for precious metals.

🧐💼 - **Provider Research:** The importance of doing due diligence when choosing a vault storage provider, ensuring transparency and trust.

💭🛡️ - **Purpose Reminder:** Recalling the core reason for investing in gold and emphasizing its protection and stability.

📜🔒 - **Storage Significance**: A wrap-up on the critical nature of ensuring your gold's safety and appreciating its historical value.

> *"To understand gold is to uncover the veiled truths of the world's economy."*
>
> *- Eminent Economic Historian*

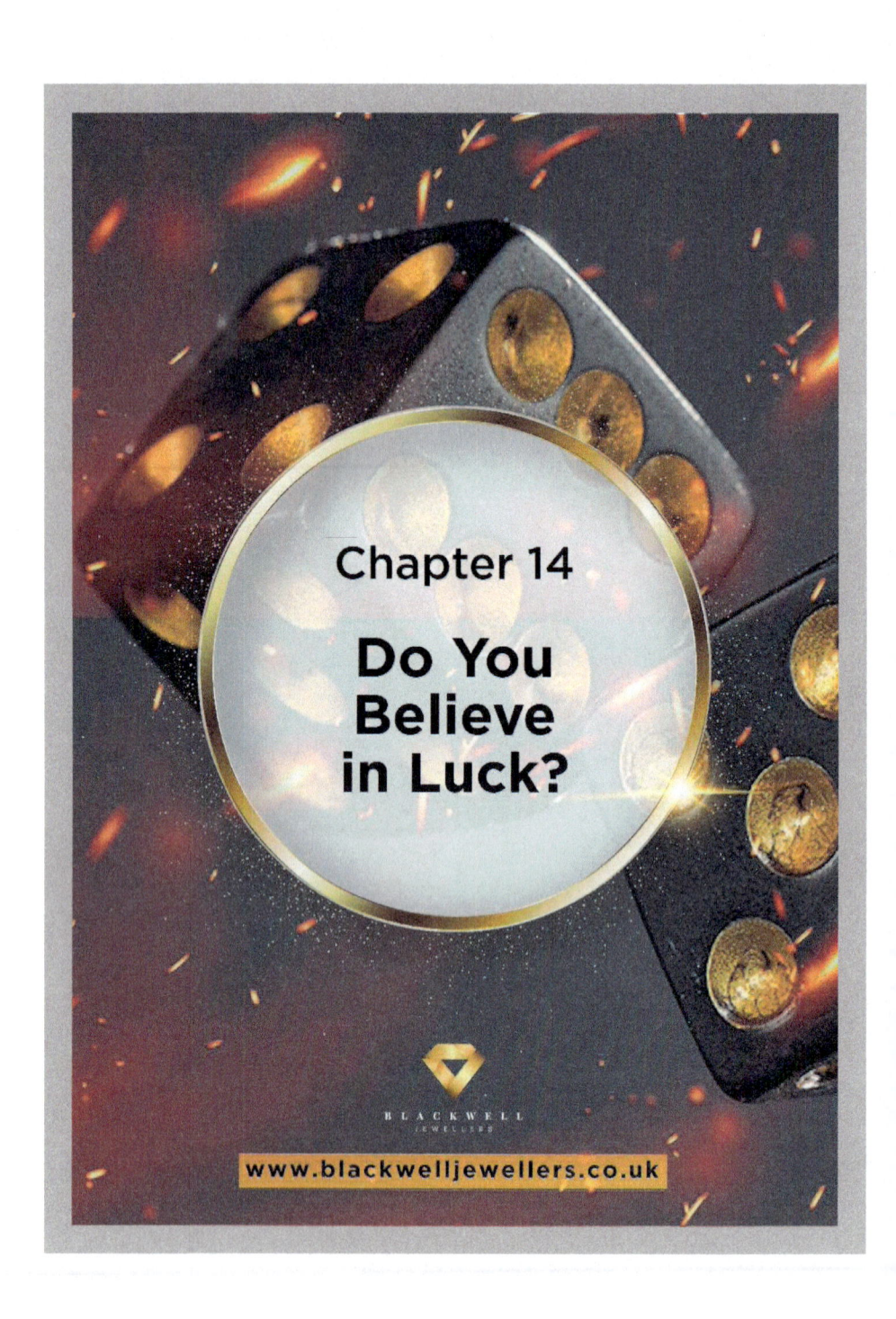

Chapter 14

Do You Believe in Luck?

BLACKWELL
JEWELLERS

www.blackwelljewellers.co.uk

"James's Fun Facts"

"If you fancy a swim, the Earth's oceans hold nearly 20 million tons of gold.

Just don't expect to find a chunk during your next beach holiday!"

Chapter 14

Do You Believe in Luck?

I'd like to share with you a story that struck a chord with me. It comes from a fantastic book called *The Psychology of Money*, penned by Morgan Housel. I've included it here because it truly resonates with my own experiences.

When I was younger, I'd often forge ahead without dwelling too much on the consequences, focusing on putting in the hard work. But sometimes hard work alone isn't enough—you need a dash of luck too.

This tale perfectly illustrates how two individuals can be in the same situation at the same time, yet luck can lead them down entirely different paths.

I highly recommend the book; Morgan does a far better job than me with this story. It offers a refreshing perspective on investing, emphasising the role of luck and discouraging snap judgements about people's successes or failures. Enjoy!

In the wild game of life, luck and resourcefulness are like two cheeky siblings, always reminding us things don't always happen just because of our own efforts.

Professor Scott Galloway had a similar idea, telling us to remember things aren't always as good or bad as they seem when looking at our own and other people's situations.

Now let's chat about a certain bloke named Bill Gates. By a stroke of luck, he went to one of the only high schools in the world that had a computer. How Lakeside School, a modest place just outside Seattle, got its hands on such advanced tech is quite a story.

Picture this: Bill Dougall, a WWII Navy pilot turned high school maths and science teacher, believed in mixing book learning with hands-on experience.

He also thought knowing a thing or two about computers would be smashing for his students once they went off to university.

In 1968, Dougall convinced the Lakeside School Mothers Club to use the money from their yearly rummage sale (about £3,000) to lease a Teletype Model 33 computer, connected to a General Electric mainframe for computer time-sharing.

And get this, the whole idea of time-sharing was only invented in 1965! As Gates later said, "Someone was pretty forward-looking."

When our mate Bill Gates was a lively 13-year-old in 1968, he met fellow computer fan and classmate Paul Allen. The two kindred spirits hit it off in no time.

Lakeside's computer wasn't part of the usual classes; it was a place for independent study, letting Bill and Paul mess around with the computer and let their imaginations run wild after school, late at night and on weekends.

During one of their late-night sessions, Allen remembered Gates showing him a *Fortune* magazine and asking, "What do you think it's like to run a Fortune 500 company?" Allen said he didn't have a clue. "Maybe we'll have our own computer company someday," Gates said. Fast forward to now, and Microsoft is worth more than a trillion quid!

Let me break it down for you: in 1968, there were about 303million high-school-age kids in the world, according to the UN.

About 80million lived in the US, around 270,000 in Washington State, and just over 100,000 in the Seattle area. Only about 300 of these bright young things went to Lakeside School.

Starting with 303million and ending with 300, these high school students ended up at the one school that had the dosh and the foresight to buy a computer.

And as luck would have it, Bill Gates was one of them.

Gates knows how important this lucky break was. "If there had been no Lakeside, there would be no Microsoft," he said.

Gates is smart, hard-working, and even as a teenager, he had a vision for computers that left many experienced computer experts scratching their heads.

But he also had a one-in-a-million helping hand.

Now let me tell you about Gates' mate who had a run-in with luck's unpredictable cousin—chance.

Most of us know Bill Gates and Paul Allen found fame and a truckload of cash through the amazing success of Microsoft.

But back when they were at Lakeside, there was another computer whizz in their gang: Kent Evans.

Kent Evans and Bill Gates became best pals in eighth grade. According to Gates, Evans was the top dog of their class. The two would chat on the phone for hours on end, so much so that Gates can still remember Evans' phone number! Evans was just as good with computers as Gates and Allen.

When Lakeside had a scheduling headache, they asked Bill and Kent to create a computer programme to sort things out. And guess what? It worked!

Kent, unlike Paul Allen, had a sharp business brain and a never-ending ambition that matched Bill's.

Kent always had a massive briefcase with him, and the pair constantly planned what they'd do in the future.

They thought about becoming CEOs, wondered about the impact they could have, and even considered roles as ambassadors or generals.

Whatever they dreamed up, Bill and Kent knew they'd do it together.

However, when Bill looked back on his friendship with Kent, his voice became sad.

They could have kept working together, gone to college, made Kent a founding partner of Microsoft.

But fate had other ideas. Kent's life was sadly cut short in a mountaineering accident before he could finish high school.

With around 3,000 mountaineering deaths in the US each year, the chances of this happening to a high school kid are a grim one in a million.

Bill Gates had one-in-a-million luck by going to Lakeside. On the other hand, Kent Evans had a one-in-a-million stroke of bad luck, never getting the chance to reach his full potential.

The same energy, the same force, but with completely different outcomes.

*

In life, there's a thing called luck, and there's another thing called risk. They're like two peas in a pod; you can't have one without giving the other a cheeky nod.

Both happen because the world is so complicated that our actions can't always control what happens to us.

With over 7billion people on this planet and countless moving parts, it's no wonder things outside our control can sometimes make a bigger splash than the things we do on purpose.

Luck and risk are both super hard to measure, and that's why folks often overlook them. For every Bill Gates, there's a Kent Evans—someone just as talented and driven, but who's ended up on the wrong side of life's game of chance.

If you respect luck and risk for what they are, you'll see that when it comes to judging people's success, including your own, things are never as good or as bad as they seem.

Now if you go around saying people's success is all down to luck, you might come across as a green-eyed monster, even if we all know luck exists.

And when you judge yourself, blaming your success on luck can be a bit of a bummer. Sure, if you're well-off, your sibling might be too, that's often true.

The quality of your education and the opportunities you get are linked to your parents' status. But find me two siblings, and I'll show you two people who don't think that rule applies to them.

Failure, which can range from going bankrupt to not hitting a personal goal, gets a bad rap too. Did a business fail because they didn't try hard enough, or were their investments just rubbish?

Sometimes that's the case.

But it's tricky to know for sure. Every goal worth chasing has less than a 100% chance of success, and risk is what you get when you end up on the unlucky side of things.

Let's say I buy a stock, and five years later, it's gone nowhere.

Maybe I made a terrible decision to buy it in the first place. Or maybe I made a smart choice with an 80% chance of making money but got stuck in the unfortunate 20%.

How can I tell?

Was it a mistake, or the reality of risk?

It's tough to measure whether some decisions were clever or not, and in day-to-day life, we usually don't bother. It's too hard.

We prefer simple stories, which are easy but can be oh-so-misleading. When looking at the story of life, look at the bigger picture, knowing luck and risk play a part in everyone's journey.

When we judge our failures, we tend to go for neat and tidy stories about goals and effort, because let's face it, we can't read minds!

"You messed up, so it must have been a bad decision," is the story that makes the most sense to us. But when we judge ourselves, we can whip up a fantastic tale to explain our mistakes and blame bad outcomes on risk.

Take the cover of *Forbes* magazine, for example. You won't see them celebrating unlucky investors who made good decisions but got the short end of the luck stick. Instead, you'll find rich investors who made so-so or even risky choices and just happened to get lucky.

They both flipped the same coin but ended up on different sides.

The tricky bit is that we're all trying to learn about money—which investing strategies work, which don't, how to get rich, how to avoid being skint.

We usually look for these lessons by observing success and failure, thinking,

"Do what she did, avoid what he did." If we had a magic wand, we'd figure out precisely what part of these outcomes were caused by repeatable actions, and what role random risk and luck played in swaying those actions one way or the other.

But guess what?

We don't have a magic wand. We have brains that like easy answers and don't have much patience for fiddly details.

So, when you're trying to learn from others' successes and failures, there's often more to the story than meets the eye.

Luck and risk play their part, and sometimes things are just a bit more complicated than they seem.

As we reach the end of this book, I'd like to share with you my own tale of how fortune and risk have shaped my journey. I believe it's crucial to remember life is full of twists and turns, and sometimes a little bit of luck can go a long way.

My entrepreneurial adventure began in the early 2000s, and by 2006, I'd managed to open my first jewellery shop. It was around this time that gold prices began to soar, reaching new heights, as I mentioned earlier.

I'd poured my heart and soul into the previous three years, scrimping and saving every penny to make my dream a reality.

However, I also had a fortuitous encounter with Lady Luck.

Merely six months after opening my store, the frenzied 'Cash 4 Gold' era kicked off, enabling me to accumulate enough capital to expand my business.

Some might attribute my success solely to luck, but I'd argue my dedication and risk-taking over those three years played a significant role in positioning me to seize the opportunity when it arose.

So, was it just luck?

I believe it was a combination of both.

This brings me to an important point: nowadays, there's a growing number of self-proclaimed gurus peddling their advice on what to buy and invest in, using their personal stories as evidence.

However, it's crucial to recognise much of their success may stem from being in the right place at the right time.

What worked for them may not necessarily work for you, and more often than not, these gurus are making a mint by selling courses rather than practising what they preach.

As I've grown older, I've become more cautious when it comes to taking risks. Perhaps because I have more to lose, or maybe it's simply the wisdom that comes with age.

Regardless, I continue to invest in gold and silver every month, firm in my belief these precious metals remain a safe haven and a wise investment.

James's Chapter Summary for the Busy Bee (Or a Quick Recap)

🚶 🍀 - Paths Diverted:

A reflection on how identical circumstances can lead individuals to vastly different outcomes due to luck.

🖥️ 🎓 - Gates' Fortune:

Marvelling at the sheer serendipity of Bill Gates attending one of the rare schools equipped with a computer during that era.

🌙 🛠️ - Dreams and Dedication:

The late nights Bill Gates and Paul Allen spent honing their skills, reminding me of similar times of ambition and aspiration.

⏳ 💡 - Ahead of Time:

Recognizing the sheer foresight of a school possessing a computer back in the 1960s and the opportunity it presented.

🌍 🌐 - A Rare Opportunity:

Pondering the odds of being among the select few who receive an unprecedented chance amidst millions worldwide.

🏔️ ❤️ - Kent's Tale:

Emotionally touched by the story of Kent Evans and the unpredictable duality of life's fortune and misfortune.

🎲🗣 - Balance of Fate

: An introspective look at how the intertwining forces of luck and risk influence and shape our destinies.

📄😊 - Behind Success Stories:

Realizing that many acclaimed stories, especially those heralded in magazines, often have an underlying current of luck amidst the effort.

🏅🎆 - Golden Opportunity:

Reflecting on my personal journey into entrepreneurship and the serendipitous timing of the 'Cash 4 Gold' era.

🗺🛡 - Navigating Advice:

Emphasizing the importance of discernment and understanding context when considering success anecdotes or advice.

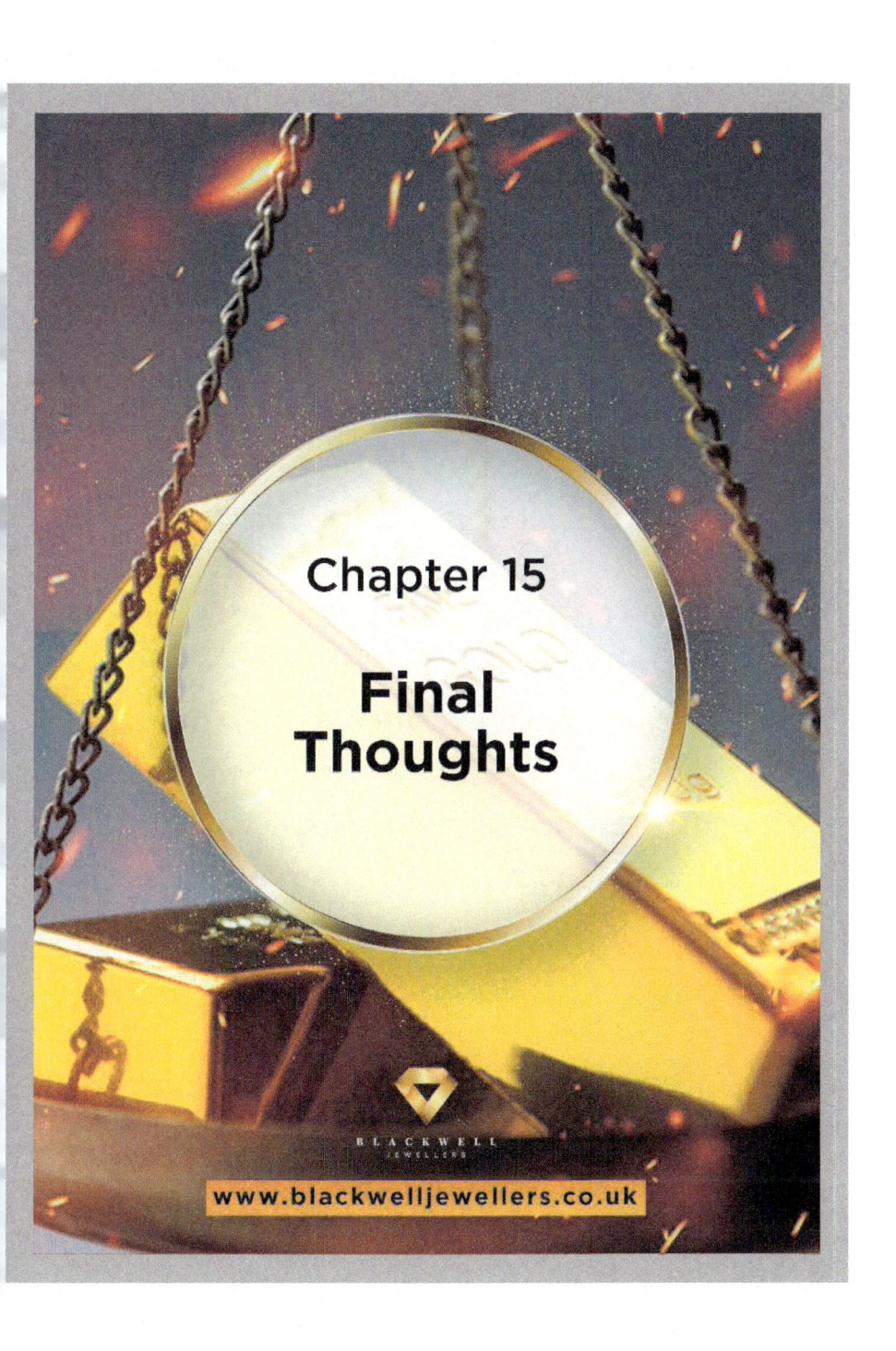

Chapter 15

Final Thoughts

"James's Fun Facts"

"History 101:

Back in the day, banks were like wild teenagers — unpredictable and always up for a party. Central banks were created to keep them in check. But over time, they've occasionally been caught sneaking out, manipulating currencies, and causing a ruckus.

Oh, the drama!"

Chapter 15

Final Thoughts

Life is a blend of hard work, calculated risks, and occasionally a touch of luck. It's essential to remain vigilant and discerning when it comes to deciding whose advice to follow. In this ever-changing world, it's vital to stay informed and make educated decisions that suit your individual circumstances.

Throughout this book, I've endeavoured to provide you with the knowledge and tools necessary to make informed choices about gold and silver investments.

My hope is that you'll take this information to heart, apply it to your own life, and ultimately make decisions that are best for you and your financial future.

I must reiterate, I'm not a financial adviser, and the content of this book is just my opinion. Always do your homework before investing in anything.

But if you need advice on jewellery, gold, or anything else in this realm, please don't hesitate to get in touch. I'd be delighted to hear from you!

So there you have it: the grand finale of our literary journey. I hope you've enjoyed reading this book as much as I've enjoyed writing it.

I hope the information and stories within these pages have entertained and enlightened. I'd like to express my genuine gratitude for your time and attention. It's been an honour and a pleasure to share my insights and experiences with you, and I hope my journey has inspired you to forge your own path with confidence and wisdom.

But the journey doesn't end here. As you venture forth into the glittering realm of precious metals, don't forget to drop by and say hello, share your successes, or seek guidance.

Together we'll continue to learn, grow and appreciate the beauty and value of gold, silver and precious metals.

So, until we meet in person or cross paths once more in the pages of another book, I wish you all the very best in your endeavours, and may you always find joy, prosperity and a touch of sparkle wherever life takes you.

Yours sincerely,

James," Your Friendly Jeweller" Marsh

"Paper money, at best, is a promise; gold, on the other hand, is a fact."

― *Esteemed Investor*

Chapter 16

A Little Gift from Me!

Dear Reader!

Navigating this book with me has been like embarking on an expedition into the shimmering depths of precious metals. We've delved into Central Bank Digital Currencies (CBDCs) and gazed at their gleam on gold investments. It's been quite the adventure, right?

But hold on! Before we part ways, I've got a little shimmering surprise up my sleeve.

Picture this chapter as a wrapped gift from me to you. No strings attached. Just a heartfelt 'thank you' for sticking around, nodding, questioning, and perhaps even laughing a little.

A Little Trip Down Memory Lane

Let's take a detour for a moment. Once upon a time, armed with passion, sheer determination, and perhaps a nudge from Lady Luck, I set out on a journey.

Fast forward a few years and now there stand three glistening stores in Kent's very heart. Gravesend, Bexleyheath, and Maidstone are now homes to Blackwell Jewellers.

And every day, inside these stores, at least three master jewellers sculpt, mould, and create wearable art.

Here's Where It Gets Exciting for You

Pop quiz!

What do you get when you combine an appreciative author and a jeweller? An exclusive reader offer, of course!

How about a FREE Jewellery MOT?

Think of it as a spa day for your bling. Plus, a bonus clean, polish, and rhodium treatment (usually that's a £49 deal). March into any of my stores, show us your sparkle, and just relax. We've got the magic touch.

Picture your cherished engagement ring, the one with stories whispered between its stones, or that family necklace that's seen countless reunions.

They might be calling out for some pampering. And trust me, the last thing we want is for you to face the agony of a missing gem. Those moments? They're heart-squeezers. Let us shield you from that.

And, because you've given this book your time and curiosity, there's an extra sprinkle of gratitude: a 10% OFF on any service or purchase. It's not a sale; it's a heartfelt invitation.

Why the generosity? Simple. I've got a hunch: One visit, one experience of our handiwork, and you'll feel the vibe of the Blackwell Jewellers family. You'll sense that unique blend of tradition, art, and warmth.

Why We Shine Brighter

Every individual at Blackwell Jewellers isn't just an employee. They're artists. In a world flooded with the ordinary, we're that little alcove that cherishes the timeless art of jewellery-making.

Also, we respect history. When so many exquisite heirlooms risk vanishing in molten pots, we offer more than just scrap prices. Each piece tells a story, and we're here to ensure these tales resonate for years to come.

If you ever ponder selling a piece, or if your eyes are set on a new gleaming friend, ping us! Dive into our digital realm at

www.blackwelljewellers.co.uk.

Remember, I'm not just a jeweller, but a mate who's keen on discussing the glitters and glimmers of this world. And, oh! Don't miss our exquisite range of 22ct gold coins. A must-see for enthusiasts!

So, from investing nuggets to rekindling old flames (of jewellery, of course!), always recall you've got a buddy in the shiny biz. Can't wait to welcome you to our family.

Cheers,

James Marsh, Owner of Blackwell Jewellers.

Printed in Great Britain
by Amazon